God Entered My Life

The Extraordinary Spiritual Journey of Charles Bozidar Ashanin

Peter Denbo Haskins

ISBN: 978-0-9859074-4-0

Table of Contents

Preface

by Theodore J. Nottingham

Dr. Charles Ashanin has left in the wake of his life on earth an extraordinary legacy. Numerous individuals of all ages and all walks of life have been touched to the core of their being by his unique agape and will carry his memory in their hearts forever.

Dr. Ashanin's great love and awareness of God gave him rare insight into the souls and spiritual needs of others. He saw and felt things of the spirit in ways that most people cannot. Though he never claimed to be so, Dr. Ashanin was a true mystic, combining an all-consuming devotion to the Presence of the Holy with gifts of clairvoyance, wisdom, and a profound understanding of Scripture and of the writings of the early teachers of the Faith. As a scholar of early Church History, he inspired many students with his genuine living out of the Gospel through his care of their souls. At the university of Ghana in Lego, African, at Allen and Claflin universities in South Carolina, and finally for 23 years at Christian Theological Seminary in Indianapolis, Indiana, Dr. Ashanin was more than a professor -- he was a mentor, beloved friend, and companion on the spiritual journey.

Dr. Ashanin's deep life of prayer and compassion also committed him to ecumenism, to the Body of Christ in all its manifestations. As a member of the Eastern Orthodox Church with twelve hundred years of Slavonic spirituality in his soul, he worked closely with students studying for the Protestant ministry, enriching their traditions and perspectives of the Gospel in the manner of a true "staretz" (spiritual guide). This ecumenical commitment cost him greatly. For its sake, he suffered the disdain and persecution of colleagues whose "modern" Christianity mocked and rejected his devotion to the ways of the early Church.

This virtual martyrdom never deterred him from caring for Christians of all traditions and he remained to the end a luminous example of the true ecumenical spirit, which is nothing less than the imitation of Christ in all aspects of life.

Born in Montenegro in 1920, Dr. Ashanin graduated from Cetinje Seminary and expected to serve his beloved Serbian Orthodox Church until he found himself on the "hit list" from both the Nazis and Communists who decimated his country during World War II. Forced to flee his homeland and his family, he eventually made his way to England and Scotland where he earned a Ph.D. from Glasgow University under the tutelage of leading theologians such as the Disciples' own William Robinson. Later he established a deep friendship with Dr. Ronald Osborn which brought him further into the ecumenical world of the Christian Church (Disciples of Christ).

Dr. Ashanin's personal impact on the people who loved him is immeasurable. Each one has a personal story of the special influence he exerted upon their mind, heart, and soul. Along with the living testimonial of his exceptional Christian spirit, Dr. Ashanin has left us with his book, *Essays on Orthodox Christianity and Church History*, along with numerous articles, his remarkable foreword to the book, *The Spiritual Wisdom and Practices of Early Christianity*, his chapter in *The*

Vision of Christian Unity and interviews in several video programs including the nationally televised "The Resurrected Life: Understanding the Meaning of Easter" and "Sharing the Spiritual Journey."

The following is a taste of his words from the introduction to *The Spiritual Wisdom and Practices of Early Christianity*:

As a consequence of God's disclosure, there comes into being the communion of the Redeemed, i.e., the saints who are the Church, not as an organization but as the Divine-human organ, the mystical Body of Christ. Therefore, the Church is not so much an "observed" reality but is a spiritually discerned reality… The agenda of the followers of this path is a journey through askesis (total surrender) in order to enter more fully into the life of Christ according to Saint Paul's saying: "It is no longer I who live, but Christ lives in me" (Ga 2:20). The pathfinders of the Way are the patriarchs, prophets, apostles, martyrs, confessors, and ascetics. This vision of Christianity centers on the person of Christ as the Axis around which their whole life revolves…. They believe Christianity to be the Revelation of God, i.e. the unveiling of the divine which unites the believer in Christ with God so that the believers may live in God and God in them.

The author Peter Haskins – friend and student of Charles Ashanin – has created a work of love with this book which will contribute to the continued legacy of this rare example of spiritual authenticity in our world. With its careful research, meaningful theological and spiritual reflection, and wonderful gathering of history, anecdotes, and timeless words, this book offers the reader a face to face encounter with a mystic whose life can still teach anyone who has eyes to see. As Charles said in his last words to me while filming *The Resurrected Life*: "Memories fade but Truth lives." Charles Ashanin incarnated Truth in a very special and unforgettable way. He lives on in spirit and blesses his friends to this day.

INTRODUCTION

It was the fall semester of 1990 at Christian Theological Seminary in Indianapolis, Indiana. I was a first year student studying for the ordained ministry. One of the courses I enrolled in during that first semester was Early Church History with a professor named Charles B. Ashanin. It was Dr. Ashanin's last semester to teach formally after forty-five years of teaching the history and theology of the Early Church. My first year at Christian Theological was his twenty-fourth.

It was mid-semester during one particular lecture that I was introduced to the multilayered universe of this seventy-year-old political and religious exile from the mountains of Montenegro. He was well-known throughout the seminary for his unusual style of lecturing. He would stand in front of his class with no notes and his eyes closed, and he would lecture in an extemporaneous manner, his arms waving about like the conductor of the London Philharmonic Orchestra. I was especially preoccupied with one matter or another, and before I was aware of anything going on around me, I was awakened as if from a deep sleep by Dr. Ashanin standing in front of me waving his arms and saying, "Wake up, wake up." I sat there, completely immersed in my humiliation, which immediately turned to anger as Dr. Ashanin said, "Come and see me in my office." He then turned and walked back to the front of the class and continued his lecture. After a week or so, I made my way to his office. He spoke to me of staying awake, yet he was not referring to physical sleep. He was referring to a kind of awareness which was completely foreign to me, what the early church called *metanoia.* He told me my time was being wasted in day dreams.

Much of the current tone within Western Civilization is characterized by a focus on specialization. Much of the focus within the West's form of capitalism--its education, even its military--is geared toward finding a niche, finding a specific talent or expertise and functioning within the society with that specialization as one's identity. It is a movement away from a collective center, splitting and dividing away from its origin. For Charles, the sign of a sick civilization is this movement away from one another in all aspects, but especially interpersonal relationships.

The sign of a healthy people being informed by their civilization and also informing their civilization is characterized by the training and development of the person first with a common philosophy based upon the value of each human personality. This common philosophy is Christian in its very nature, a deep appreciation for, and reverence of, the holy element within each individual person. Without this belief that human beings are "unrefined particles of Christ," as Teilhard de Chardin describes it, the equation cannot be solved. Each human being is treated as holy. Specific, personalized attention to the talent of each personality is an essential part of the educational process. Each personality must develop in its own space and time. A truly functioning Christian civilization is one which gives its members space to develop their full potential. For Charles, all Christians are related by their basic mission described in the New Testament, namely that all Christians should be supported and defended. One of the keys to a vital Christian civilization is "solidarity within its ranks." Christians must support one another in order to maintain an atmosphere conducive to full development of human beings. This does not give a Christian civilization permission to become warlike. It should be protective in nature. Charles felt this to be a fine line, one which needed to be attended to collectively. He felt no need to defend God; rather, he believed that it was correct to defend Christian civilization, which can give us space to become the human beings God intended.

With this as an underlying philosophy of education, the civilization then draws its strength from the developed energy of the many. The civilization draws everyone to the center, not the other way around. The civilization's energy is gathered, as in Christ's feeding of the five thousand (Mt 14:13-21). This, in effect, insures a common respect for the person and his or her political rights. There is a common philosophy of humanity. This method of "drawing inward" not only conserves energy for a civilization, but also creates new energy, all in one motion. For Charles, this is how a civilization protects itself from decay, by developing the person through a commonly held respect for the holiness of the individual.

Coming into harmony with the Divine Spirit is a personal choice. He felt that the matter of freedom was essential to the development of the human individual. If someone forces you into a certain form of spirituality, that use of force is little more than a kind of terrorism, which in turn makes God a terrorist. Christian civilization is an attempt to *humanize* humanity--"like leaven in the dough."

The spiritual dimension to human existence is the key to Charles' understanding of Christian civilization. It is the root equation for true humanism. It combines the Greek method of education known as the *Paideia*, and the theology of *Theosis* contained within early Christianity. Charles saw the Early Church Fathers, especially St. Basil the Great, St. Gregory of Nyssa, St. Gregory of Nazianzus, St. Maiximus the Confessor, St. Symeon the New Theologian and St. Gregory Palamas, as the theologians who expressed clearly the proven wisdom of the Byzantine Civilization. Charles saw, through the study of the history of Byzantium, a key to healing our collective illness. As a professor, Charles made use of a philosophy of education and of humanity which differed sharply from those of his *host* community. His methods and philosophy behind those methods were on another plane than those of his peers.

Thus, he was often misunderstood by colleagues, peers, and administrators who assumed his paradigms of education and culture, theology and politics were similar to their own. They missed a key aspect to understanding Charles Bozidar Ashanin: He was on a mission. In order for his mission to be completed, it must be fulfilled in his time and his own terms, which intermingled with the attributes of his personality. He may have moved to and lived in America since 1960, but he was not an American. He remained identified with another time and another place, with a civilization which survived and flourished between 312 and 1453 C.E. His life and his spirit were fed by the collective energies of the saints of that era. His story is really about this ancient energy being released through him into the universe around him. Here is his untold story.

Notes to the Introduction

1. Ashanin, Charles, "Turning Toward the Light." video interview with Theodore Nottingham, 1988, transcript p 4.
2. Velimirovich, Nikolai, "The Serbian People as a Servant of God." The Free Serbian Orthodox Diocese of the United States and Canada, Grayslake, IL 1988, p 9.
3. Ashanin, Charles, "Christianity and Humanism." Crane Review, Crane Theological School, Tufts University, Winter 1962, p 99.
4. Ashanin, "Christianity and Humanism." p 102-103.
5. Ashanin, "Christianity and Humanism." p 103.
6. Ashanin, "Christianity and Humanism." p 103.

Prologue

Kolashin, Montenegro, January 6, 1942 "Pasje Groblje."

On Orthodox Christmas Eve of 1942, approximately a thousand Communist Partisans attacked the Serbian Chetnik-controlled Kolashin, Montenegro, a villiage of 3,000 inhabitants. The Chetnik forces, greatly outnumbered, withdrew from Kolashin. In an effort to institute their policy of liquidating "class enemies," the Communist Partisans began patrolling the streets announcing that none were to leave their homes or immediate executions would begin.

Under orders from chairman Savo Brkovic of the Communist court martial, a stray dog was taken to a field in the neighborhood of Kolasinski Lug. In the middle of the field they placed a "Badnjak," which is a traditional Serbian yule log tied with straw and oak leaves.[1] Brkovic's men nailed the dog to the Badnjak and named it the "Graveyard of Dogs," or "Pasje Groblje."

The Partisans proceeded systematically to arrest "class enemies." They moved from house to house, singling out doctors, lawyers, officers, teachers, civil servants, judges and priests. On the evening of January sixth, under the light of burning torches and the sound of the crucifying dog, over three hundred and fifty of these class enemies were executed with hammers. During the executions, the Partisans gathered the surviving members of the village in a high school auditorium and forced them to take part in a "People's Feast," which included songs and dancing, a sort of anti-Christmas.[2]

On his escape following the Communist takeover, Charles Bozidar Ashanin visited Pasje Groblje in the village of Kolashin. In his unpublished autobiographical novel, he writes, "I stayed in Kolashin for a few days waiting for some news of transport to take me to Cetinye. I went to see the infamous monument to Communist terror, 'the dog's graveyard.' To my relief the Chetniks had dug out the bodies of the Communist victims and reburied them in a common grave in [another] part of the town. I went to the place to pay my respects to their memory. The place was tended with due care. There was an inscription on the cross marking the grave: 'To the martyrs of Communist tyranny.'"[3]

Notes to Prologue

1. Ashanin, Charles. "A Garland for a Mother." Unpublished, p 140.

2. Fleming, Thomas. *Montenegro: The Divided Land*, Chronicles Press Rockford, Illinois, 2002, pp 136-137.

3. Ashanin, Charles. "A Garland for a Mother." p 265.

Part 1

Histories

Remembrance of Self

The story of Charles Bozidar Ashanin should begin in his own words, telling his own story. Here is an excerpt from a 1988 taped interview with Ted Nottingham entitled "Reflections on the Meaning of Easter":

> This is the first time I remember myself as a human being. We lived in the country. There you don't have running water in the house, however distant it was, and my mother, I don't think . . . uh, she was afraid to leave me at home. It was evening; it was Autumn, probably September, and she took me by the hand and took the pitcher to get some water. We were going around this path and over there . . . we plant fruit trees, and the plums were, the branches were overladen on this path, and I pulled myself up to pluck some of those, and she said,

"Oh no, you can't do that!" And I said, "Why not?" She said, "They don't belong to your grandfather" (where we were living, which would have been all right); "they belong to your uncle, and you didn't ask him."

Original sin! I said, "Mother, nobody sees!" And she was stunned. I mean, this little urchin, this first time I remember myself as a human being, manifesting the original sin. And she just stood there, totally stunned that this manifestation of original sin could come from that urchin. And she said,

"But Child, God sees." This was the first time I heard the word *God.*

But the way her whole response and impact of that was such that I said, "God? Who is this God?" And I looked, and it was evening, and the . . . you have been in France; I don't know how it is there, but the Mediterranean sky is a beauty to behold because it stands with stars, and uh, on a beautiful evening this overwhelming cosmic experience, like jewels! And I looked at these . . . and I can't explain

> it, but this reality that she named as God, he was there! It was, uh . . . I mean he was not a bogey or . . . but something splendorous, something beautiful, something . . . her words authenticated my own awareness of this reality, and so God entered into my world, and I can't get rid of him![1]

It is appropriate that the story of Charles Bozidar Ashanin begins with a scene from his early childhood with his mother in the Mojkovac countryside of Montenegro (then a part of Yugoslavia). It was this land from which he was born the eldest son of seven children. It was also the land he left in April 1945 as a political and religious exile, at age twenty-four, to escape the hammer blows of Tito's Communist Partisans. He would never return to his family or his homeland.

This is the story of one man's struggle to become fully human as God intended in a world mixed with good and evil. With this struggle came distance, physical and psychological, from his family, friends, co-workers and country.

To be fully Montenegran means to be a synthesis of a rich ethnicity and religious heritage. To be Montenegran means to be intensely Serbian as well as Christian Orthodox. This reality carries with it enormous weight for an individual, especially if this individual is the eldest son. The family, the clan, the country, the religion, the history, all call upon those sons to continue the fight against the Turks and the Huns, no matter the cost. To the Montenegran, there is no higher calling in life than the glory of self-sacrifice for the greater good of the Serbian people. William Jovanovich writes in his book entitled *Serbdom*, "...that if a man is not willing to yield his comfort and risk his body for a purpose greater than his own mere day-to-day survival, then he cannot finally know the meaning of his own life."[2]

It is within this milieu that Charles Ashanin was born, raised and grew to manhood. Yet in the name of Christian Humanism and Apocalyptic Spirituality, Charles would abandon his primary identity as a member of the Asanin clan from Montenegro and seek his cosmic identity as a son of the Light (John 12:36)[3] This is not simply a story of political and religious exile from twentieth century Eastern-European Communist tyranny. It is a story of how one man's exile shaped his relationship with his God and the world around him.

The life of Charles Ashanin gives us a rare glimpse into the activity of God within a human heart and the impact that activity can have. With this force comes newly created life, forged in the furnace of faith. This faith cuts us loose (Mt. 10:34) from the people and ideas which prevent us from developing freely as a human beings. This faith becomes a battle, the battlefield being the fallen psyche (Genesis 3:22-24) of anyone who has ears to listen (Luke 8:8). Charles was among those people who listened and heard too much to turn back. For him there was no forgiveness if he turned away (Luke 9:62). He could not get rid of God because God revealed to Charles an ontological secret: God does not carry a passport. God is not Serbian or Turkish or American; God rises above this world of good and evil. Nevertheless, God is fully invested in this world, beckoning his children back to the Light (Revelation 3:20).

Some children answer this call, yet it unleashes energy. This energy is not designed to bring entropy. It is designed to be a catalyst, a transforming element. This new energy requires a new type of attention in order to retain, to conserve. Christianity is about this attention, which ultimately leads to permanence, salvation. It is about union. To some, this cost toward union is foreign, easily demonized through personalization. Yet to others it is the moment of liberation, long anticipated and rumored in brief moments of clarity in the depths of the inner heart.

Notes to Remembrance of Self

1.Ashanin, Charles. "Reflections on the Meaning of Easter." audio interview with Theodore Nottingham, November 1998.

2. Jovanovich, William. "Serbdom," Black Mountain Publishers, Inc. Tucson, AZ 1998, p 86.

3. For reason of self-preservation as a political and religious exile, Charles added an "H" to his last name shortly after leaving Yugoslavia. Later in Britain, he changed his first name from "Bozidar" to "Charles" for similar reasons. He writes in a 1998 journal to his daughter Valerie, "And while I was renamed Charles in Britain by my English friends--instead of being called by my Serb name "Bozho"--this was to protect me from being easily discovered by Tito's agents and murdered by them on suspicion of being counter-revolutionary." p 49.

The Surprise Twin

Charles Ashanin's profession on earth was that of historian, and his life mirroed the history of the twentieth century. He was making the passage from adolescence to adulthood at a time and place where the fury of Balkan Nationalism clashed head-on with Aryan Nationalism and Slavic Communism. As in 1914, the Balkans were again the flashpoint in 1941 for the major powers' practice of geopolitics at the expense of native populations. The two world wars of the twentieth century serve as macabre bookends to Charles' early life.

Not much is known of those years. He was an exceedingly private person, never given to telling anecdotes about his childhood. Yet in a set of extraordinary audio interviews recorded between September 27, 1999 and February 24, 2000 (His death was on March 1, 2000.), his dear friend and publisher of a book of his essays, Robert Coalson, captured a tremendous amount of information in Charles' own words regarding his early childhood, as well as theological and political perspectives he held. These are cited herein as the Coalson Interview.

Bozidar Asanin was born in Iskoci, Montenegro. Montenegro at the time was a part of the fledgling union of Serbians, Croats and Slovenes known as Yugoslavia, which had been formed in 1918.

He was born on November 15, 1920. His mother, however, insisted that his birthday be celebrated on December 15. He was the younger of twins, an unexpected arrival at the home of Radosh and Mileva Asanin. An upturned saddle served as the cradle to accommodate this unexpected second son. Charles would have two sisters, Kossa and Stoya, and two other brothers, Dushan and Michael. A third sister named Smiryana would die in infancy. His twin brother died at an early age (probably five or six) of diptheria.

His father was injured in the first world war, having lost two fingers and an eye. Charles admired his father and the work he did supporting his family, yet the two great influences on Charles were his mother and his father's father. Coalson Interview 11/4: Charles expresses how much he admired his mother, but he adored his grandfather. His paternal grandfather was his link to his past, his ancient Montenegran past.

His grandfather passed on the sense of legacy to Charles, the importance of seeing himself as a descendant from Montengran royalty. His grandfather told him that his maternal great great great grandfather had been a chieftain of a Montenegran clan. To be a chieftain, especially during the occupation by the Turks, implied a great deal of warrior instinct and leadership abilities. According to Charles, "the whole [Montenegran] people were an army." Charles' grandfather was determined to keep the tradition of Montenegran royalty alive. He picked Charles to be the future standard-bearer; the mantle would fall to him one day.

Charles speaks extensively (Coalson Interview 11/4) of his early education through the Montenegran tradition of epic poems. The Serbian people were oppressed under the rule of the Ottoman Empire for over four hundred years. In order to preserve the memory of their people in the shadow of occupation, they began an oral tradition, a ritual reciting of their story, especially their defiance of Muslim rule. With a one string instrument called a "gusle," a storyteller called a "gusla" would sing to the gathered children and adults, thereby passing on the tradition of this proud but oppressed people. These Homerian poems urged the children, including Charles, to "never surrender" in the face of even overwhelming odds. He tells Bob

Coalson that it was through the epic poems that he learned to be "hard headed about my freedom being usurped."

The education given by the gusla gave Charles a sense of his own dignity and made him feel connected to a cause that was quite large, perhaps even large in the universal sense. The teaching was not just about defiance. It stood within the framework of Christian civilization, stressing the importance of human remembrance. Charles learned that by remembering God's activities through a people, one can thereby remember God's activities through oneself. As one remembers God's activities through oneself, one recalls who one is in relationship to God. In Coalson Interview 10/12, Charles says, with Socrates, that we human beings are trying to remember the transcendent wisdom already given to us. We came from the will of God and are meant to be in union with God's will. This concept of our pre-existence continued as a theme throughout Charles' life. In the same interview he says, "There is something more than earthly about our existence." He believed that emigrants like himself who dream of their homeland are effectively projecting their feelings upon their homeland and their ancestors, inchoate feelings derived intuitively from their pre-existence. Charles expresses this interplay between transcendent origins versus historic origins when he described this proclivity of emigrants as "the projection of the metaphysical upon our hereditary traits." Early on Charles was taught, "we are not self-made; we are a mosaic."

His grandfather fell asleep in 1942. Charles was twenty-two years old. His grandfather had made a remarkable impact on his life. Early on he determined to keep alive the royal tradition in Charles by insuring that he received an education. Charles did not know why his grandfather chose education as the path, other than that he felt that it was a way to overcome the treatment by the Turks. The Turks treated the Serbs as property, unfit for education. Therefore, he wanted Charles to at least graduate out of the level of poverty. He originally wanted Charles to be an "exciseman," yet Charles performed so well at school that early on he became the teacher's assistant.

During Coalson Interview 11/4, Charles describes himself as bookish by nature, but also due to his physical size. Charles was not tall enough or powerful enough to compete physically with his peers. He talks of being teased about his short stature by bullies. Yet this only brought out his defiant nature at an earlier age. He would never lose this edge.

His grandfather was the one who sent him to grammar school. The secondary school was too far away, so his aunt allowed him to stay with her in order to continue his education. It was in secondary school that Charles truly began to discover his love for history; there he was introduced to the literature of the Serbian People. He speaks of being heavily influenced by the Serbian poet Njegosh who introduced him to the classics of European literature--French, Spanish, German, but mostly Russian.

Njegosh opened Charles' mind to Golgol, Pushkin, Tolstoy and Dostoevsky. Their words resonated with him as a Slav, but also on a more cosmic level as well. By the time he finished secondary school he had read extensively and broadly. He was eighteen years old and searching for an intellectual guide, a mentor. During the conclusion of studies at the secondary school, he came into contact with his "aunt's nephew," a law student at Belgrade University. In him he thought he had found his hero. However, visiting a friend of his cousin in Belgrade, he learned that his cousin was an atheist and a communist. This proved very disillusioning for Charles and ended their friendship. His search for a guide continued.

Charles gives special recognition to an unnamed clergyman who gave him a sense of who he wanted to become. He was a teacher of religion at his secondary school. Charles describes the teacher as intelligent, with background in culture and education similar to his own. He was a refined human being, someone the boy felt was "who I would like to be." Due to the influence of this teacher, Charles decided to attend Cetinje Bible College where he studied for the next six years to become an Orthodox priest. Admission to Cetnije was not easily accomplished. Charles had to compete in order to be accepted. To his grandfather, this showed him he had been right about Charles; he was a leader.

It is important to put this period of Charles' life in historical context. Charles would become an historian of the Early Church. As an historian he had an understanding of the human component of history. To him, history was not an abstract study of chronological lines and theories of cause and effect. History was created by struggle, the struggle of humanity attempting to evolve out of its fallen, animal nature. Civilization was in essence an experiment in human evolution.

Author Robin Amis says that Christianity was chosen as the official religion of the Eastern Roman Empire in 312 C.E. due to its civilizing effect. It provided individuals with opportunities to develop emotional maturity. This moral cohesion had a unifying effect on the civilization as a whole. A civilization, says Amis, functions to its potential when it provides the proper atmosphere to develop the human to their potential. Therefore, there is a symbiotic relationship between the individual and the civilization itself. For civilization to be functioning properly, the individual needs to be functioning well.

Charles understood and appreciated the value of a functional civilization. He experienced firsthand the uncivilized, fallen nature of humanity through the historical lens of twentieth century geopolitics in the Balkans. It is here from within the crucible of an oppressed Balkan people that a lion-hearted individual, Charles Bozidar Ashanin, emerged.

The Christodule

In the preface to "A Garland for a Mother,"[1] Charles gives a "moral and spiritual rationale . . . for the existence of historians." He writes,

> The trouble about history is that it is written by conquerors who falsify it by making it into propaganda glorifying their deeds, which are often misdeeds and crimes against humanity. It is for this reason that the historical truth is difficult to come by because the most important witnesses, the victims of the conquerors cannot be interrogated and their side of the story told, for the conquerors often see to it that incriminating evidence against them is destroyed by flame and sword . . . But thanks to the mysterious something I shall call the still small voice of conscience, the universe prevents history from accepting the verdict of those who say that *might is right*. It instills in the

> mind and hearts of the more sensitive spirits of humanity a reluctance to accept the propaganda of the conquerors as true history. It inspires in them a passionate urge to seek for the truth in order to find out what really happened in history beyond the account of the conquerors.[2]

With his philosophy of history as a signpost, we begin by briefly discussing the general history of the Serbian peoples in the Balkans from a Serbian Orthodox perspective. In his work, "The Serbian People as a Servant of God," Bishop Nikolai Velimirovich presupposes the synonymous link between the Serbian people and the Orthodox faith and Church. He writes,

> the most basic belief of the Serbian people is their belief in *sudba*--not in blind fate, but in a providential, planned, and just destiny . . . A Serbian proverb says: *Nema smrti bez sudjena dana*--"There is no death except on the destined day." This has made the Serbs brave and fearless, for the most basic belief of the Serbian people is their belief in destiny.[3,4]

A knowledge of this paradigm is essential in understanding anything regarding Serbian faith and history.

Serbian history as viewed from a post-communist, post-holocaust, Western perspective is often myopic. The "question of the Serbs" must be initially understood from looking at the Serbian cosmology. Ultimately, the Serbs do not see themselves as just names on the historical scroll of European history. They view themselves and their entire history as having eternal consequences. They live and sacrifice in this world with a belief that their actions here have eternal ramifications. To the Serbs, they are an historical people who are on a collective mission as a *Christodule* or servant of Christ. Yet to Bishop Velimirovich, as he regards it, throughout their eight hundred years of known history as a people, the Serbs have consistently violated their role as servant of Christ. They consequently suffer disastrous defeats as they seek to fulfill their mission as servants of God.[5]

Yet this link is implicit and strong, even if it often serves the purpose of pure, secular Serbian Nationalism. William Jovanovich writes,

> to be a Serb is to be Orthodox, if not today, then yesterday. We are a people whose national identity

> is intertwined with our Church; and this truth persists wherever we may live . . . Serbs earned their independence by fighting against foreign rulers and by adopting their own faith. Surely, they cannot forget how early their church became coincident with Serbdom.[6]

Notes to The Christodule

1. Sometime in the mid 1970's, while Charles, Natalie and their four children were living in Indianapolis, IN, he was contacted by his mother's aunt. She was living in "a northern city in the United States" and had recently made a journey back to Montenegro, where she had visited with Charles' mother, who told her about Charles and where he was living. His great-aunt, now inspired by the knowledge of his presence in the United States, invited him to visit her. This was the first physical meeting with a family member since his exile in 1944-45. The tangible result of this visit was an autobiographical novel by Charles entitled "A Garland

for a Mother." During the writing of this work, Charles discovered a cathartic outlet for expressing his emotions regarding his exile. In this rare glimpse into his person life, Charles offers a detailed account of the four years which preceded his exile and the historical and personal events which led to his decision to leave family, clan and country.

2. Ashanin, Charles. "A Garland for a Mother." p 1.

3. Velimirovich. p 7.

4. Charles expresses similar philosophy in "A Garland for a Mother"; "April 1941. The Greeks knew how to name this sort of universal demoralization, despondency and collapse. They call it *moira*, fate! But the frightening thing about it was that the unnamed had a face and the face was menacing, terrifying and ugly. Its name was Hitler and Nazi Germany." p 7.

5. Velimirovich. p 11.

6. Jovanovich. p 91, 92.

Montenegrans as Serbs

The relationship between Montenegrans and Serbs needs some examination. There is no possible way to deal with this subject in a complete way given our context. We shall try to offer a concise version, shedding some light on the historical milieu for a Montenegran born in 1920. The relationship between Montenegrans and Serbs exists symbiotically, yet at the same time it is diverse and complex. They share a collective history in their struggle against the occupying powers of Turkey and Austria-Hungary over the course of four centuries. They also share the galvanizing effect of this oppression coupled with the influence of Orthodox Christianity upon them as a people. The Montenegrans and Serbs have been allies in their struggle to remain a separate entity for centuries of geopolitics. In this sense, Montenegrans and Serbs identify themselves as Serbian, yet they are still separate peoples: Montenegrans are Serbs, yet Serbs are not Montenegrans.

Many of the Slovenes, Croats and Serbs of the Balkan regions are of Slavic ancestry. They migrated in the sixth and seventh centuries from what is today Northern Germany and the Baltic Sea region.[1] Yet there are no ancient peoples who are the genetic contributors to the inhabitants of the Balkans. According to Thomas Fleming, "all of the Balkan people are a mixture of stocks: Illyrian, Dacian, Pannonian, Greek, and Celtic, as well as Germanic, Slavic and Turkic." [2]

With this shared genealogy, history and religion, we will focus now on some key events in Serbian history, with a narrowing focus on Montenegro during World War Two. Ironically, it was a move away from the Christian Orthodox center in Constantinople which began the first Serbian Kingdom in modern-day Montenegro. In the year 1036 C.E., a man named Stefan Vojislav renounced his allegiance to Constantinople and pledged loyalty to Rome. The neighboring Serbian tribes started to join together, and by 1077 they had formed a Serbian Kingdom called *Zeta.* [3] Around 1166 a key historical figure came on the scene whose name was Nemanja. He founded an Orthodox Christian dynasty that would last for two hundred years. Nemanja is credited as the father of eight centuries of Serbian history as a Christian people. [4]

However, the process of Christianization among the Slavs of the Balkans goes back to the first years following the ministry of Jesus of Nazareth. Paul reports in Romans 15:19 that he preached "even into Illyrium," while Titus was in Dalmatia (II Timothy 4:10). Yet the Christian culture was slow to assimilate with the "primitive" or native belief system. In a fascinating passage, Charles refers to this pre-Christian culture in "A Garland for a Mother" when he writes

> The occasion demands that every *paterfamilias*, as the head of his family, assumes the duties of a priest and presides over the Christmas Eve festivities. Although the intent and content of these are centered on the gospel narrative of Christ's birth, there is also much pre-Christian ethos included. This is evident in the Yule log fire, which is reminiscent of the old Slav worship of the god Perun, the most high god of heaven, whose symbols were the divine fire and light. His altar was the hearth of every home, and it is around it that the whole celebration takes place. [5]

The pre-Nemanja Christianity in the Balkans was actually more of a political compromise than a faith conversion of a people, no matter how gradual. This appeasement of the Byzantine Empire ended when a young and Catholic Nemanja was imprisoned in Constantinople and was converted to the Orthodox faith. When Nemanja came to power in 1166 as Grand-Zhupa (equivalent to a royal king) he was very thorough in his conversion of his people to Orthodox Christianity, while maintaining amicable relations with the Catholic Church. [6] In a further case of irony, the Orthodox Byzantium that Nemanja was establishing in his newly formed Serbian Kingdom, was captured and demoralized by the Venice-based Crusaders during the infamous Fourth Crusade in the thirteenth century. With Constantinople sacked, their empire began to crumble and other rising powers were able to expand and strengthen their borders. It was during this period that Nemanja and his son, Saint Sava, began building churches and monasteries which would serve as the foundation of Serbian identity during the four centuries of Turkish occupation. While the Byzantine Empire suffered a major defeat, the new Orthodox state in the Balkan rose to prominence. Along with the Greeks, they helped defend the crumbling Byzantine Culture. [7]

Once the Nemanjic Empire began to crumble, a Turkish threat began to loom. Initially there was a Serbian defeat at Maritsa in 1371, then inroads were made by the Turks at the Battle on the Kosovo Plains in 1389. The Turks began to take control by 1459 and by 1521 the entire Balkan region was under Muslim Turkish rule when the Fortress of Belgrade was finally captured. [8] It was at this time that there was a massive migration of the Serbs to neighboring parts of Europe. Many were taken captive and transported to the newly conquered city of Constantinople (1453) which had been substantially weakened a century and a half earlier by the Christian occupying power of the Fourth Crusade. [9,10]

For the next four hundred years the Serbs were a working class people in an obscure Turkish province. They had experienced a brief two-century period of independence, yet now they were in an obsequious relationship to the occupying Ottoman Empire. The Muslim Turks were true to the teachings of Mohammed in so far as they did not force their religion upon those they conquered. The Serbian people were allowed to worship their Christian deity. In many ways this was a form of rebellion for the Serbian People in that Orthodoxy was their main form of Serbian identity. It was during these years of Turkish occupation that cemented the Serbian national identity with that of Orthodoxy.[11] Carrying on the tradition which began with Nemanja, the Orthodox Church was the only Serbian institution under the Turkish occupation. Orthodoxy and Serbia would forever be synonymous.[12]

Notes to Montenegrans as Serbs

1. Judah, Tim, "The Serbs; History, Myth and the Destruction of Yugoslavia,"

Yale University Press, New Haven and London, 2000, p 7.

2. Fleming, p 18.

3. Judah, p 9.

4. Veliminovich, p 12.

5. Ashanin, Charles, "A Garland for a Mother," p 140.

6. Spinka, Michael, "A History of Christianity in the Balkans; A Study in the Spread of Byzantine Culture Among the Slavs," The American Society of Church History, Chicago, IL, 1933, pp 77-79.

7. Spinka, p 90.

8. Laffan, R.G. D., "The Serbs; The Guardians of the Gate," Dorset Press, New York, 1989, p 21.

9. Ashanin, Charles. Unpublished letter to George Stephenapoulous, Sept. 14, 1995.

10.Ashanin, Charles. Unpublished journal written to his daughter Valerie, 1998, p 46 where Charles writes of the legend that many Serbian nobility escaped to Montenegro after the defeat at Kosovo, establishing Montenegro as the center of Serbian Aristocracy.

11. Laffan, p 23.

12. Judah, p 17.

A Contextual History of Serbia, 1918-1945

It was not until 1878 that Turkey finally recognized Montenegro as an independent state. Prince Nikola led Montenegro into a brief period of statehood, that resulted in becoming a constitutional monarchy by 1910. [1] In 1912, Montenegro and Serbia, along with Russia joined to liberate all the Balkans from Ottoman control in what was known as the Balkan Wars. The prospect of an independent Balkan state was a minor yet potent reason for the major powers going to war in 1914. By then, all of Europe was caught in the historical continuation of geopolitics: war.

By 1918, although defeated and their government of King Nikola in exile, Montenegro was on the victorious side of the peace table. Yet by the end of the year they had lost their identity and had become a part of the Kingdom of Serbs, Croats and Slovenes formerly known as Yugoslavia. This dream of a united Kingdom of Southern Slavs was noble and optimistic, yet destined for failure. The ethnic and religious differences were so deeply ingrained in their history that it was essentially a forced peace. The Croats and the Slovenes were historically Catholic, while the Serbs were Orthodox Christians and the majority of the Bosnian population was Muslim. From 1918 to 1941 these ethnic and religious tensions seethed underneath the outward appearance of a unified Yugoslavia. This unity was largely in the name of safety against the ever-present powers of Austria-Hungary, Germany and the aging Ottoman Empire. Each member of the Yugoslav union had a deep mistrust toward the other (with the exception being Montenegro and Serbia), with each member fostering the idea of independent statehood.

As Adolph Hitler and the Nazis rose to power in Germany and Austria in the 1930's, Yugoslavia faced a stark and menacing old enemy. Hitler himself blamed the Serbs for starting World War I. So by March 1941, the Axis Powers declared war on Yugoslavia. Charles begins the prologue to "A Garland for a Mother" with this passage,

> Who can forget it? The place was Cetinye, the capital of Montenegro, once a Balkan Principality but at that time a provincial center of the Kingdom of Yugoslavia. The date was March 27th, 1941. The Rector of our College stood on the platform as we

students took our places in the auditorium where we had been summoned for a *special* announcement. He was motionless like a statue, a typical Montenegran, tall and gaunt, dressed in the black cassock of an Orthodox priest, over which hung a silk mantle fastened by the medallion and chain of his *Alma Mater*, Moscow Theological Academy, from which he had graduated before the Bolshevik Revolution. The Very Reverend Rector, Michael Vuisich, had a grey beard which gave him a patriarchal appearance, and the grave bearing with which he carried himself, enhanced his personal and official authority. We knew that something important had happened and that it had to do with national fate, for everybody knew that somehow Yugoslavia would renounce the pact [Axis Tripartite Pact] which Prince Paul and the Yugoslav Government had concluded with Hitler's Germany. The rector motioned to us, indicating that he was about to speak. We all turned into a solid body of silence for we wanted to hear every word. There was no public speaking system to carry his words, and the hall, once a billiard room for the Episcopal Palace, left much to be desired acoustically. He sensed the tension of silence which added to his own emotional strain, and we saw how for the second time he failed to master his emotions and give us '*the news*'! This only made the atmosphere even more charged with apocalyptic forebodings. "Tzar Lazar and Kossovo are again upon us, and the time has come again for our country to make a choice as it did then," he began. We looked at each other. The metaphor was well chosen for it invoked the most awesome event in the history of the Serbs, the destruction of Serbian freedom and state by the Ottoman Turks at the end of the fourteenth century, when the Serbian prince Lazar met Sultan Murad and his horde on the plain of Kosovo.We knew who the new Sultan was and the new Turks whom he led in assault of the freedom of the whole of Europe! The Rector after a pause continued:"I am happy to tell you that our people have rejected the pact with the new Attila and his Huns! The new government led by King Peter II has now been formed, and we have cast our lot as a people of freedom or death, instead of slavery. Long live the King!" We went wild with enthusiasm. All of us had lived since

> Hitler's coming to power in Germany under the shadow of terror which he inspired. Now the fear of Hitler had become a direct threat, and its face was staring at us. We were confronted with it and felt relieved because now we could defy it openly, come what may.[2]

Initially the Montenegran government signed an appeasement called the Tripartite Pact. On March 27, 1941 there was a coup which renounced the Tripartite Pact.

Berlin immediately declared war on the entire Balkan region. The Serbs and Montenegrans were no match for the Axis Powers (along with the Croats) all of Yugoslavia was soon occupied.

On June 22, 1941 Germany invaded the Soviet Union. With this invasion the Communist Party of Yugoslavia entered the war. In short, this marked the beginning of a civil war within Yugoslavia, with both sides resisting the Axis occupation. Montenegro was placed under the jurisdiction of the Italian military. The Communists, led by Josip Broz Tito, were known as the Partisans. The Serbian loyalists were known as Chetniks. The Nazi Croats were known as the Ustasha. The message of the Chetniks was largely one which appealed to the conservative Serbian peasantry regarding restoration of a Serbian state.[3] The

Communists were much more politically savvy and spoke to the entire population of the former Yugoslavia. Their message was one of unity of the entire population with freedom for all people. 4

In the name of national and Slavic unity with the embattled Soviet Union, the Partisans began a systematic cleansing of the population. This cleansing was not based on ethnicity. It was based on ideology. Thomas Fleming writes,

> Long before the war, the Yugoslavia Communists knew that to establish a Communist state would require the murder of hundreds of thousands of people: rich businessmen, of course, but also peasants who owned a few acres, convinced royalists as well as Marxists who had joined Stalin's party, to say nothing of priests, civil servants, and anyone who displayed the slightest capacity for independent thought. The Italian occupation of Montenegro and the subsequent uprising gave Communists the opportunity to begin the massacre under the cover of wartime exigency, and by the end of the war, they and the Ustasha had gone a long way toward purging Montenegro (and the

> whole Serbian nation) of "reactionary element," though there were still a few survivors to be dealt with.[5]

During the initial stages of the war and on through D-Day itself in France in June of 1944, The Chetniks were under the impression that the Allied Forces would invade mainland Europe through the Adriatic corridor. The fact that it did not happen was a betrayal by the Allied Powers which led to a demoralization among the Chetnik ranks.

This demoralization was a complete rout on the psyche of the Serbian Chetnik movement when in the early Fall of 1944 Yugoslavia was invaded by the Soviet Union. The Chetniks were completely defeated. All was lost to the independent-minded Tito and the Yugoslav Communist Party which was a different beast altogether than the Soviet Communist Party.

Montenegro, in the meanwhile, melted into the atheism of post-World War II, totalitarian Yugoslavia. This was essentially another form of occupation. Pax Tito. In "A Garland for a Mother," Charles gives a personal account of one of these "reactionary elements" which the Partisans attempted to eliminate in order to pave the way for a postwar Communist state. The Partisans were ruthlessly objective in their feral approach to cleansing the population of any embodiment of conscious thought or independent action. The Balkan tradition of clan revenge which began with the Nemanjic Empire was now taken to new depths. The entire population of Yugoslavia was one clan, now feeding upon itself.

If Charles had stayed in Yugoslavia, he most assuredly would have been murdered for his level of education and/or his religious beliefs. The Orthodox faith and tradition of the Serbs (as with the Russian people) was an issue the Communists sought to overcome by whatever means necessary. Religion was now of the Party, not of God. During Coalson Interview 1/18, Charles says that he did not hate the Communists because of their system of government or economics. Rather, he hated the Communists because of their atheism. For them their atheism was a form of religion.

The Communists came into Yugoslavia as the liberators of the people from the German Nazis. They attempted to recruit Charles, yet Charles knew that if he joined out of a sense of survival and he murdered anyone, he would be automatically ineligible for the Orthodox priesthood. Charles was a pacifist even before he witnessed all the atrocities of the war. Yet the war and his subsequent exile convinced him on a deep level that pacifism was his only true option. In Coalson Interview 11/18,

Charles describes a time when the Partisans were trying to intimidate him into joining their ranks. Charles refused even to salute them. When the commander asked Charles why he did not salute them, Charles replied, "I have not learned." To that the commander returned, "We will teach you."

Charles began to deal existentially with his own mortality, becoming reconciled to his own death. At this time he began to search the scriptures, finding tremendous comfort in the passage from the fourth chapter of Acts, verses one through 22, where Peter and John are arrested by the Jewish Council and imprisoned. They reply to their captors that it is right to obey God and not man. This seems to have been a major clue for Charles as to his next move.

Charles tells Bob that when WWII started, he immediately left Cetinje and returned home to his mother and father. He speaks of his father briefly in Coalson Interview 12/10. He says that he was not close to his father, who in his semi-invalid state was very withdrawn and shy. Charles interpreted this as his father not wanting to show himself as weak nor wishing to defend himself like a wounded animal. He knew his father loved him even though he was distant from him. Charles was told that when his father died, he called out, "Bozidar, where are you? Why are you not here?" Following his death, his father appeared to him in a dream as a young man, giving Charles a kiss.

Charles lived with his family for six months in fear as the Partisans roamed the countryside fighting the loyalist Chetniks. The Chetniks briefly took control of the area. The remaining faculty at Cetinje asked the Italians, who were in control of the Yugoslavia, for permission to reopen the seminary. This permission was granted, and Charles returned to school for a welcome respite from the chaos of war. This lasted only nine months; the institute finished its agenda and all the students returned home.

In "A Garland for a Mother," Charles speaks of the Montenegran qualities of fearlessness in the face of death and the belief in a fierce loyalty toward one another in the face of oppression. Yet Charles witnessed his fellow clansmen and kin sink into the condition of fallen humanity. In the name of independence and freedom, that same spirit was being extinguished by an overwhelming brutality unleashed from the collective human spirit. By 1944 it was obvious that Charles had lost his confidence and respect for his countrymen. He writes, "My disappointment with my fellow countrymen verged on bitterness. I thought them to be at least a humanized group far above the level of barbarism. I excused all I saw the Communists were doing because I blamed it on the poison of the Communist indoctrination. But though the symbols were different--one group exalted Stalin and Tito, the other the King in exile--they were made of the same stuff, for they were both walking on the brink of barbarism.[6]

It was at this time that Charles asked God either to allow his flight from Yugoslavia or to take his life. He felt that even if he survived he would have to change his whole being. In Coalson Interview 1/18, he says he felt that his exile was like being frostbitten before he was ripe. He regretted that he was not intellectually and emotionally mature enough when his exile came upon him. He says to Bob, "I was homeless, stateless and helpless."

Charles, at the age of twenty-four, moved from the idea of God as freedom, to the knowledge that God is freedom. And that freedom requires sacrifice. Yet he also understood that this sacrifice is not always that of the physical body. It can also be about the sacrifice of illusions which we hold in our minds, the influences of family, community and training. Charles sensed that he was more than an Asanin, more than a Montenegran. His life held personal worth that demanded recognition and preservation.

In "A Garland for a Mother," Charles writes about his farewell meeting with his younger brother Dushan. Charles tries to explain why he is leaving in spite of the impression of cowardice his actions may suggest. Dushan asks about the meaning of understanding;

> Understanding is, Dushan, that above everything else beyond our mothers, our parents, our homeland, these beautiful mountains around us, beyond our ancestors, our church, everything, everything, even our own lives, we belong to God first and foremost, uniquely, unreservedly, and absolutely.[7]

Yet there was a price, a unique death which occurred quite gradually. In a revealing letter to the editor of the *Washington Times* dated August 6, 1992, Charles asks then Governor Bill Clinton to be pro-Serbian in his Balkan foreign policy if he is elected to the presidency. He writes,

> I am of Yugoslav origin, from that part which has survived the breakup of the country. I left Yugoslavia and my family in April of 1945 because I did not want to live under Tito's terror. My family

was not that fortunate. Recently my brother [Dushan] and I met in Switzerland after 50 years of separation. Tito and his communist gang put him in one of their most terrible gulags for 6 years and destroyed his health and his family. Two of his children died while he was being tortured, as were countless others, at *Goli Otok*, in what is now Croatia. His crime was in having a brother who refused to submit to Tito's terror. I was overjoyed not only to see him alive but to see that he had maintained his dignity and decency in spite of the terrible inhumanity of Tito's communists.[8]

Notes to A Contextual History of Serbia; 1918-1945

1. Fleming, p 109.

2. Ashanin, Charles, "A Garland for a Mother," p 1-2.

3. In 1941, Serbs comprised 40% of the total population of Yugoslavia.

4. Judah, p 120.

5. Fleming, p 150.

6. Ashanin, Charles, "A Garland for a Mother," p 256.

7. Ashanin, Charles, "A Garland for a Mother," p 263.

8. Ashanin, Charles, unpublished letter to Bill Clinton, August 6, 1992.

Interlude; Freedom and Martyrdom

". . . the worst form of enmity: the destruction of one's freedom."

— from "A Garland for a Mother"

As the Serbian people were slowly enveloped by the Ottoman Empire beginning in the fifteenth century, a significant development occurred in the collective identity of the Serbs. As has been said previously, their freedom of religion remained largely intact. Yet, as with any occupying presence, the cultural, political and economic freedom of the indigenous population was an initial casualty. Their cultural, political and economic identity was now being absorbed into an empire. In the milieu of an empire, the foundation is essentially that of domination. The empire maintains control through a cultivation of fear and intimidation. This fear causes the formation of an identity within the dominated which is characterized by obsequiousness. This identity is that of a servile people, not a free people. Therefore, any grasp of or grasp toward freedom can be the lifeblood of a captive people. The Serbs took advantage of what freedom they had and forged a new identity, beyond the scope of the occupation with all its baggage. In addition to the traditions within their faith, they formed this new identity through their art, with rich traditions being born through epic songs and poetry about their military and religious heroes and heroines.

Charles had a rich understanding of the importance of freedom for a people and for individuals. Freedom poses itself as a foundational element within the cosmology of an oppressed people. This is expressed beautifully for the Slavs through the prophetic voices of writers like Dostoevsky and Berdyaev. The Serbian people fought to keep this concept of freedom. As oppression and the struggle for freedom within the Ottoman Empire intensified, the form for this fight for freedom quickly began to take another form, that of martyrdom. The Christian religion bases itself historically in martyrdom with the historical figure of Jesus of Nazareth. Jesus is followed in martyrdom by all of the Apostles (with the exception of John who survived his Patmos exile and died of natural causes) and countless followers of The Way during the first two and one half centuries of early church history. Yet this martyrdom is historically unique in that there was the resurrection of Jesus, with the hope of resurrection to follow for those genuine believers.

As the Serbian people lost more and more freedom, their lost identity was made new by the identification with the death and resurrection of Jesus Christ. There was the belief that Serbia was not dead, only awaiting its resurrection. Serbia had experienced an honorable death at the hands of the Turks and was only in slumber. Within the structure of their new identity, a Serb was given the choice of an honorable death in the name of God, clan and country. This death was chosen in order to remain free from the oppression of the dominating power and to open oneself to God's grace.

Yet martyrdom can easily evolve from a free choice in the name of God, clan and country, into a mighty and unmanageable ally, its appetite insatiable. What begins in a drive to remain free to worship and evolve, can quickly turn into an issue of bravado, machismo, reinforced by patriarchy. The religious motivation fades away, and all that is left is this demand for an honorable death, with no room to choose another way to preserve freedom. If someone chooses not to die with honor in order to obtain the freedom to evolve, then labels of dishonor appear. Either way, a death occurs.

The Call of the West

Charles had a first love. Her name was Mila. She died from a gunshot wound to the leg from either a Chetnik or a Partisan. According to the "Garland" text, this seems to have been the final event which convinced Charles to leave Montenegro. He now had no true allies left to assist him in his resistance against both Partisans and Chetniks alike.

In a revealing story he told Bob during a conversation that was not audio-taped, Charles tells of the time when he was leaving his family's home, on his way to the Adriatic coastline. He was walking along a wooded path, terrified and uncertain who he would meet. Suddenly he came upon a rabbit, which was startled to the point that the animal jumped up into the air and landed in Charles' open coat. There the animal began to burrow its way deeper into Charles' vest, as if Charles were himself safe haven from some predator. Charles says that it was then, in a moment of grace-filled clarity, that he realized he wasn't to seek refuge, but rather to *be* refuge.

Returning home from his nine months at Cetnije, he found the situation had worsened. The Partisans had gained strength and momentum. It was then that he asked the Bishop permission to go a monastery at Praskvitza.

The first glimpse he had of an Allied-assisted exit was with a wounded Italian soldier at the beginning of the war. He was a Waldensian from Northern Italy who had studied in Edinburgh, Scotland to be a Protestant minister.[1] Charles gave him refuge from the Partisans and Chetniks at his own risk. He was very drawn to the Christian and British connection with this Italian soldier. This British connection would be a lifeline.

Charles now felt imprisoned living at home in Italian controlled Montenegro, with the Communists becoming more of a danger with each passing day. Charles (even at the urging of his parents) decided to leave. Yet he had no idea where to go or how to get there. The prospects of a job in Montenegro were almost nonexistent. Then, during a BBC broadcast from London in 1944, he heard of British intelligence contact with the Chetniks along the Adriatic coastline. He had heard a rumor of an Abbot at a monastery near Budva on the Adriatic coastline who was a British agent. He decided to leave home and travel to Budva, then hopefully to Northern Africa where the Allies were in full assault against the Axis Powers.

This was the last time he would see his mother alive. It was during his time of departure that their home was nearly hit by an Allied bomb, targeted at the retreating Germans. As he and Dushan left, they found every crossroads bombed beyond recognition.

Dushan accompanied him to Kolasin, where they parted. He hitched a ride on a truck going to Padgoritza, then to Centinye. When he arrived in Cetinye he visited Bishop Yoanikije, the Metropolitan of Montenegro. He asked the Bishop for permission to stay for a while at the Monastery of Praskvitza. During his visit with the Bishop, he had a disillusioning conversation with this man who appeared to Charles as more of a politician than a man of God. This encounter was important because this was the last psychological "crutch" which Charles had remaining. He had now made a complete separation: no longer did he equate his view of God with that of the Orthodox Church, the Serbian people, his Montenegran clan or his immediate family. These illusions were being stripped from him by the brutal circumstances of a civil war wrapped up within a world war, with the participants groping in the twilight for new gods.

His time in the Monastery of Praskvitza was one of recuperation and preparation. He appointed himself monastery cow herder. This was propitious due to the fact that it gave him time to read. This would turn out to be a monumental time in his life as he prepared to head straight toward the unknown, the West. He found a treasure trove of world classics in the library of the parish priest of Budva. He discovered the genius of Fyodor Dostoevsky, his ability to expose and elucidate the problems of evil within the human condition. His reading of Dostoevsky's complete works was a key event in Charles' intellectual evolution. At a time when his psychological buffers were being torn down all at once, he needed an emotional and intellectual direction. Everywhere he turned, his life revolved around risk. There was no safe port toward which he could turn. He needed an internal beachhead where he could lay claim to some new ground and defend it. Ironically, on the Allied-bypassed Adriatic coast of Budva, Montenegro, Charles had found within himself the tiniest foothold where he might start over.

He tells Bob a story about a trip into town from the monastery in order to get a haircut. Although Italy by this time had surrendered, there remained in Yugoslavia Italian soldiers. Charles was next in line, with an old man and an Italian soldier waiting behind him. The Italian soldier was cleaning his gun. Charles decided to allow the old man to go in front of him when it came his turn. Soon after the old man sat down, the Italian soldier's gun discharged its element, finding its way into the old man's stomach. The old man died two days later of the gunshot wound.

He heard news of an opening as a reader at the monastery at Podtastva where there was rumored to be two former Yugoslav naval officers waiting to sail to Italy when the Allies invaded. He found the Navy officers, and they made an agreement to allow Charles to go to Italy with them if and when they sailed. He was destined never to make his escape across the Adriatic. Charles received word from the naval officers that they were ready to sail. Yet after he arrived at their rendezvous, there was an unknown Italian who convinced the officers to take him instead of Charles. The Italian promised them many rewards after they got to his homeland. They left without him, leaving him stranded on the Adriatic Coast. A few years later, Charles and his new bride Natalie met one of these Yugoslav Naval officers who had abandoned him. Natalie tells the story of meeting him in a cathedral in New York City. To his relief Charles had survived, noting that Charles had always been on his conscience. He further reported that the Italian who had taken his place, once arriving on Italian soil, had immediately disappeared, giving nothing in return.

In an article for the "Russian Orthodox Journal" in May, 1967 entitled "Guns in the Catacomb," Charles describes the weeks which followed his disappointing abandonment. It was November of 1944. Charles decided to join the Yugoslav Nationalists or the Chetniks who were camped near Progoritza. He describes the cold rain, the overwhelming sense of doom which hung over the camp, yet also a sense of defiance in the face of the Partisan momentum. He was at the camp for three weeks when they received the order to march toward Bosnia. Charles decided to visit a small hermitage in the vicinity which had been founded by a well-known aesthetic named Father Simeon. The hermitage had a catacomb-like chapel with elaborate icons painted on its walls. Charles had wanted to visit the chapel for holy communion early on the morning of their departure. When he reached the hermitage, he discovered that the monk in charge had retreated with the Chetniks, fearing for his life. He met a young woman named Zagorka whose family was temporarily living in the hermitage. He found out that her fiancé was a good friend of his, so he decided to stay for lunch, not only to see him but also to feed his half-starved body. During lunch, Zagorka's brother arrived. He was a Chetnik on his way to Bosnia as well, and strongly urged Charles to wait for him so that they could travel together.

Charles was very reluctant to stay, sensing great danger if he did. Yet he interpreted this voice as the voice of fear, and he decided to stay the night. Two more Chetniks joined them, and they settled in for the night. At about 10 p.m. they heard loud bangs on the wooden blinds as the Partisans were yelling for them to surrender or the house would be burned to the ground. The four men made their way through the passageway in the hermitage (which had been dug out of the rock by the hermit) toward the chapel. He and a drunk man he called the "exciseman" hid in an alcove where the body of the hermit lay in rest, as the Partisans began searching the hermitage. Two Partisan officers made their way toward the chapel with "pistols, daggers, and short machine guns," and began shouting into the darkness for them to surrender. He and the exciseman were armed with their own guns. There was danger from both sides because the exciseman was quite drunk, completely frightened and unpredictable. He had the choice of surrendering and almost certain execution or trying to shoot his way out of the chapel. It was at this moment that he sensed his own violation of the sacred space. The Partisans had two hurricane lamps with them which lit the small chapel. The frescoes and icons on the walls loomed large, suddenly giving Charles a foreboding sense. He felt that not only were the Partisans trespassing on sacred ground, but he too was trespassing. The icons seemed to speak to his soul, what he called a "terrifying reality, a thousand times more real than the Partisans, my friend, I and our guns." He sensed the presence of the old hermit there in the chapel, holding the chalice of the Lord's Supper. Whereas a few moments before he had felt the compassion of the Lord as he looked upon the icon, now he felt the anger of the Lord and realized that God's power to judge toward heaven and hell was far greater than the power of the Partisans to kill the human body.

He writes,

> I put the rifle against the wall. I felt a deep release. Something in me of the greatest importance was solved. I said to my companion, "Stay where you are, do not move." As I moved toward the guerillas, my eyes caught a fresco depicting Christ and His disciples in the storm, in which Christ was commanding the storm to be still. In my agitated state this had a tremendous effect upon me, for it had a very personal meaning. I called out and surrendered to the Partisans. They rushed toward me, holding their machine guns against my forehead.[2]

As they were exiting the chapel, Charles was "filled with an irresistible force, and I pulled myself free from the hands of the guerilla and ran forward." Under the volley of gunfire and hand grenade blasts, Charles ran for cover in some rocks and soon lost consciousness. When he came to, the Partisans were still close by, but their footsteps soon faded off into the night. No one had been captured.

Charles makes this significant reflection on the incident, giving us clear insight into the source itself of his understanding of the world and his place in it;

> I felt helpless. There in the catacomb my pursuers had had an advantage over me, for it was the sacredness of the place that had disarmed me. Then a sense of disgust with my hunters came over me. I remembered their blasphemies in the catacomb. I recalled all the things which divided me from them and realized that we were two worlds in conflict, without compromise. To be killed by them did not appear as tragic as having to live under them . . . I was glad I had not desecrated it with blood, even that of my would-be murderers. I realized that the deepest thing which divided me

> from these Communists was just that for me there was something higher and more sacred in which I believed and they did not.
>
> I felt the Sphinx of life had answered me its riddle, and in no way did I feel cheated that at twenty-two my life might have its end. I realized that I was on the verge of grasping a great secret, and the secret was Christ, in Whom our existence touches the transcendent realm and becomes part of it. His words, "Put your sword into the sheath, for he who takes the sword shall perish by the sword," were spoken to me so clearly in that little catacomb that I had to obey them.[3]

After the escape of the Yugoslav Naval Officers, the German Intelligence got wind of their escape and of Charles' involvement. Charles was brought in for interrogation. He was questioned by a certain German officer who was about the age of his father. Charles tells Bob that he spoke to this officer in his native tongue, which probably saved his life. The German officer had pity on Charles, for he could see he was an innocent young man. He said to Charles, "We have killed many people like you, but I will let you go. Be very careful." He allowed Charles to escape to Italy on foot.

Veselin Kesich was a fellow Serbian exile who, by May 1945 was also in a Displaced Persons Camp. The Allies placed exiles such as Charles and Veselin in camps located in Austria and Italy. Veselin does not remember meeting Charles until after they moved to Dorchester, England in January of 1947, but recalls what life was like in the DP camps. Veselin writes, "Life in the camps was not conducive to cultural or educational outreach. We lived in near-prison conditions. The DP's gave lectures, performances, etc. and they were able to organize activities with the camp, studied languages." [4]

All those slated for theological studies in England met at a special camp toward the end of 1946, and by mid January of 1947 twenty-five to thirty Serbs were on their way to Dorchester College in England. They were taught by Serbian professors, plus two English teachers who taught them the English language and early church history in English. Professor Veselin Kesich, who went on to earn a Ph.D. from Columbia University, has this recollection of Charles during their time at Dorchester, "Bozho (as we called him then) attended all these classes and displayed great interest in them. He was grateful for the opportunity to study after a long break during the War. He became quite an Anglophile, as his accent attested. I remember that he was kind to those he came in contact with. He always tried to be positive and to see the other person's point of view. During the years we spent together in Dorchester, I do not remember him gossiping about others or criticizing his colleagues or professors. He never engaged in polemicizing." [5]

Charles needed out of Italy, and God answered him: Britain. The Anglican Church saw the ramifications of the collapse of Yugoslavia into Communism. In what was to be called the Christian Missionary Enterprise, the Anglican Church mobilized and began to search for Christian survivors from Yugoslavia who might be potential candidates for the Anglican Priesthood. From these Displaced Persons Camps in Italy they chose those with potential. Charles himself was in Rome when the Anglicans recruited him. On January 27th, 1947 Charles and many other survivors arrived in Britain. They were met by the Anglican Bishop of Gibraltar who made the final decision. Charles was one of the chosen. However, some of these were immediately chosen to go to America for training. Charles was not among this group and this caused him to feel abandoned in Britain.

Those who remained in Britain spent their first summer in the homes of Anglican Vicars. Charles was sent to the home of a Vicar by the name of Dudley Whitman. He was a bachelor in his fifties, who was very compassionate toward the twenty-six year old exile. At this time he was just getting acquainted with the English language (now his seventh language) and the new culture into which he had been tossed. Yet Dudley Whitman knew that Charles needed more guidance. He decided to send Charles to see Dr. Charles Raven for advice as to his next step.

From 1932 to 1950 Dr. Raven was the Regius Professor of Divinity at Cambridge University. From 1938 to 1948 Dr. Raven worked tirelessly for refugees from the continent. According to his biographer F.W. Dillistone, he was especially focused on finding employment and university placements for academics new to Britain.[4]

In a book review of Dillistone's work in "Encounter" and later published in Charles' book *Essays in Orthodox Christianity and Church History*, Charles writes glowingly of Raven's professional, personal and spiritual influence on his life,

> Raven befriended me after political exile from my own country [and] brought me to England in 1947. It was largely through his moral support that I was

> able to remake my own existence, dramatically overladen with the experiences of Nazi occupation, Civil War and the final Communist takeover of Yugoslavia, the country where I was born and educated during the first two and one-half decades of my life. But more than that I was seeking a Christian intellectual framework for the understanding of human history, which so recently had shipwrecked me onto the Western, English-speaking world, culture which was almost new to me. I realized that I needed to rely for my guidance and the remaking of my life upon those intellectual minds in my new homeland which, though indigenous and rooted culturally in its soil, had to be capable of catholic intellectual and religious sympathies. [7]

It appears Charles Raven was instrumental in giving Charles evidence on an existential level that indeed there were still human beings alive on the planet who could be trusted. Dr. Raven gave Charles the confidence needed to continue his exile in the same fashion that he began it. Charles continues on in the review of Dillistone's work as if it were actually a letter to Raven himself,

> Raven was my friend, to whom I am indebted greatly, for he assisted my rescue from the historical calamities which befell Eastern Europe during and after the war. Without such help as his, I was in no state, physical or mental, to cope with the demands of university graduate work in a country whose language I hardly knew. By lending me his friendship, he placed me in the world where many were his friends, and this created a psychological and intellectual environment for which I am deeply grateful.[8]

Upon arriving in Britain with the group of refugee students, the Church of England assisted them with a study program at Dorchester College near Oxford. It was here that he began the task of learning the language of the West. One of his (as well as the entire group of students) first mentors was Dr. Nicholas Zernov, who was teaching at Oxford at the time. He came to lecture at Dorchester and was a role model to Charles and the other students for his personal history as an exile from the Soviet Union, as well as his studies at the University of Belgrade. Dr. Zernov gave Charles confidence that "it is possible to sing the Lord's song in a strange land!" The first book Charles read in English without the help of a dictionary was Dr. Zernov's *St. Sergius, Builder of Russia.* [9] At this time Dudley Whitman asked Dr. Raven for advice as to the next step for Charles. Dr. Raven advised that he go to Woodbrooke College to further orient himself. Woodbrooke was a Quaker Center where Charles continued his growth and orientation. His next move was a crucial one. He went to Selly Oaks Colleges to continue his studies. Selly Oaks was the center of the Christian Missionary Enterprise. On their faculty were two men who would play an important role in Charles' life. It was here that he met Arthur Curtis and William Robinson.

In the introduction to Charles' book of essays, Dr. Ronald Osborn writes of Charles' subsequent study at Selly Oak Colleges in Birmingham, England. He writes,

> At Birmingham he came to Selly Oak Colleges, where British nonconformists had brought together a unique concentration of theological scholarship. Years later he would speak with gratitude of these Protestant teachers and students who had received him, not as a penniless alien or confessional outcast, but as a Christian brother.[10]

His time in England and Scotland was essential to his evolution. Just as Dostoevsky had given him an internal foothold on freedom, now the English and Scots were giving him a geographical center where he could begin to develop intellectually as well as emotionally and socially. Charles would forever have a deep sense of love and respect for the people of the British Isles for having accepted him without reservations when he had nowhere else to go. In a 1973 letter to Dr. Maurice Creasey, Director of Studies at Woodbrooke College (which was a part of the Selly Oak Colleges), Charles speaks highly of the institutions where he started his academic and theological career in the West. He writes, "I have always been deeply appreciative of what Woodbrooke and the Selly Oak Colleges have done for me. When I left Woodbrooke in 1949, I received a Bursary from the Dr. Edward Cadbury Fund when I studied at Glasgow for three years." [11]

In a letter of thanks to Dr. Elton Trueblood in September of 1974, Charles writes that he was a student at Woodbrooke College in Birmingham, England in 1948-49. He remarks of Woodbrooke's "splendid ministry to the world" in its support of international students.[12]

Arthur Curtis had strong connections to the University of Glasgow, and through his loving influence Charles studied for his B.D. degree starting in the fall of 1949. By the time he received his B.D., he had made the decision to remain in the Orthodox Church, as a layman, not as a priest. This was a major decision because the Orthodox in Britain were almost nonexistent at the time. By now he felt that he was intellectually and emotionally mature enough to remain Orthodox in such an environment. His next step was to continue his education on the graduate level. He had originally received a scholarship to continue his studies at Hartford University in the United States. This was during the era of McCarthyism in post World War Two America, and subsequently visas were being denied to anyone who had been born behind the iron curtain. In the meantime, he was awarded the Faulds Fellowship to study at Glasgow University. He had already received his diploma from the Eastern Orthodox Theological Seminary in Cetinye, Montenegro, which he described to Bob as the equivalent of a Bible College in the United States. He earned his B.D. degree from Glasgow in 1952, and in the summer semester of 1954 Charles studied under Karl Barth in Basel, Switzerland. Here is a letter of recommendation from Barth:

> Mr. C.B. Ashanin studied here in Basel during the summer semester of 1954. He was a regular participant in my lectures on [dogmatics] and also a member of an English colloquium. He distinguished himself through his strong intellectual contribution and an ability to quickly absorb new ideas. Because I have spoken to him on many occasions, I can attest that he is a responsible man who I believe has both the ability and the requisite qualities to become a teacher of theology.[13]

By 1955 he had earned his Ph.D. degree in Divinity from the University of Glasgow. His dissertation was entitled, "The Christian Doctrine of the Holy Spirit with Special Reference to Eastern Orthodox, Roman Catholic and Reformed Teaching." In that same year he accepted a position as Assistant Professor of Religion at the University of Ghana, West Africa. He taught at Ghana until July of 1960 when he became Associate Professor of Philosophy of Religion and Chairman of the Department at Allen University in Columbia, South Carolina. He was at Allen University for five years before moving to Claflin University in Orangeburg, South Carolina, for another two years. Both of the institutions he taught at in South Carolina were established to educate African-Americans.

Charles was a perfect fit for the milieu of an African-American institution in the unreconstructed South of the 1960's. He had an empathic relationship with the African-Americans and with their second-class citizenship status in a society purporting freedom, justice and liberty for all. Yet he knew firsthand their struggle toward humanization, toward becoming full individuals, as well as a class of people with pride and dignity.

Education was the key component in his own development as a human being. Therefore, education was also the key for African-American citizens in the white dominated South. In a February 14, 1966 letter to the Editor of the *Christian Science Monitor*, Charles is extremely tactful, yet direct, in his defense of the academically maligned African-American educational system of the 1960's. He is responding to an inference in an editorial which claimed that a student who graduated from Claflin is at a freshman level when compared with a graduate from a college in the north. The reason for this disparity is claimed to be due to their disadvantaged background and the overall economic and academic disadvantage of an African-American institution. Charles emphatically disagrees with this assessment on empirical grounds: He witnessed high quality academic performances from his students. He makes the claim that if they had similar resources to those of more privileged colleges, they would have surpassed them academically. He speaks of the struggle to rise above these innate injustices within American society. He writes, "the need, intelligence, and courage of our students is such that our struggle is also a very great privilege." 14

During these years he continued his theological training. For a semester in 1957 he was a visiting scholar at Princeton Theological Seminary. In 1964-65 he was a Lilly Post-doctoral Fellow at Harvard Divinity School. Sometime in 1956, an Orthodox Bishop named James Toombs introduced Charles to a New Yorker named Natalie Otldelnoff. They became acquainted as pen pals while Charles completed his first year of teaching at the University of Ghana, West Africa. Natalie was an American citizen whose parents were Russian refugees who barely escaped the Bolsheviks in 1918.

By 1957, Charles had been accepted to teach the fall semester as a visiting scholar at Princeton. He was intentional in applying for this position in order to be close to Natalie. He wanted their friendship to grow and knew that geographical proximity was essential. Charles courted Natalie from August through December of 1957. They were preparing to marry before Charles returned to Ghana, but Natalie had reservations about moving to West Africa and away from family. They continued close contact during the following year, and by August 1958 Charles was back in New York. On September 21st they were married at the Russian Orthodox Cathedral of Our Lady of the Sign in New York City.

They honeymooned for a weekend in London, followed by a week in Rome on their way to Ghana. The options for future employment were now open to Charles in America. He would be automatically eligible for a visa now that he had married an American citizen. Their plan was to move to the United States in order to be close to Natalie's parents. In addition, there were limited options for an Orthodox scholar to find employment in the British Isles in the 1950's. They decided to move to the United States as soon as Charles' contract expired at the University of Ghana. While in Ghana they spent the summers in his adopted homeland, Britain. It was to Cambridge that Natalie returned in May of 1960, followed by Charles in June, to prepare for the delivery of their first child, Lydia, born in September of that year.

In 1960, Charles, Natalie and Lydia sailed from Africa to Norfolk, Virginia. By May of 1962, while they were living in South Carolina, Marina was born. Just prior to their move to Indianapolis, Valerie was born in June of 1967. Their son Michael, the youngest, arrived in July 1970. Their loving marriage lasted for forty-two years. Charles considered Natalie an extension of himself. His love for her had great depth. He considered her his most important ally in his life and in his struggle to fulfill his calling. Indeed his mission would have looked far different had it not been for Natalie. One may surmise that his mission might well have failed altogether without her constant love and support. She shared him with the world. Even a *Christique*, a particle of Christ, requires a stable context in which to make itself manifest.

Ex nihilo, Charles had become a world traveler and scholar. From 1945 through 1967, Charles lived and thrived in diverse cultures: Italy, England, Scotland, Switzerland, Ghana, the American South. In 1967 he accepted the post of Associate Professor of Early Church History at Christian Theological Seminary, Indianapolis, Indiana, receiving tenure in 1973. Here he would continue to teach until his retirement in December 1990. There was much about his time at CTS that was significant, that was awe inspiring. But it was rarely peaceful.

Notes to The Call of the West

1. The Waldensians were the earliest group of organized Protestants.

2. Ashanin, Charles. *The Russian Orthodox Journal* May 1967, p 5

3. Ashanin, Charles. p 6

4. Kesich, Veselin, electronic mail letter to author, August 10, 2004.

5. Kesich, Veselin, electronic mail letter to author, May 30, 2004.

6. Dillistone, F.W. *Charles Raven; Naturalist, Historian, and Theologian.* Eardmans Publishing company, Grand Rapids, MI, 1975, p 304.

7. Ashanin, Charles. *Essays in Orthodox Christianity and Church History.* Broad Ripple Laser Type, Indianapolis, 1990, p 279.

8. Ashanin, Charles. p 283.

9. Ashanin, Charles. p 224.

10. Osborn, Ronald E. Introduction to *Essays in Orthodox Christianity and Church History*. p 2.

11. Ashanin, Charles. Unpublished letter to Dr. Maurice Creasy, undated, approx. 1973.

12.Ashanin, Charles. Unpublished letter to Dr. Elton Trueblood, September 1974.

13.Barth, Karl. Letter of recommendation for Charles Ashanin after completing a 1954 summer course with Barth in Basel, Switzerland. Letter translated by Marina Ashanin, electronic mail letter, June 27, 2004.

14.Ashanin, Charles. Unpublished letter to the Editor of the *Christian Science Monitor*, February 14, 1966.

Part II

ROLES

The Mystical Laborer

On September 1, 1967, Christian Theological Seminary welcomed Charles Bozidar Ashanin as a new member of its faculty. As an Associate Professor of Early Church History, he was hired on the basis of his training as a scholar at Selly Oaks and Glasgow, as well as the diverse, ecumenical background that he brought to the life of the seminary. Charles brought an experience of the three sides of Christianity, with an equal understanding of the theological foundations underlying each branch. [1] He also brought with him a sense of hope and excitement in the same ecumenical tone which he experienced on his warm arrival and acceptance in England and Scotland. He hoped that Christian Theological, with its sharp, ecumenical focus was in store for great historical accomplishments. [2] Yet he also had a sense of caution. In an April 12, 1967 letter to Dean

Ronald E. Osborn, Charles writes, "I feel that my joining your faculty is both an act of venture in faith and a challenge and I pray for the help of Him by whose spirit we are daily sustained that together we may work toward making CTS a veritable tower of light in the spiritual, intellectual and moral sense . . . " [3]

His connection with Christian Theological is intimately connected to his friendship with William Robinson during his studies at Selly Oaks. Professor Robinson was an Anglican who had joined the Disciples of Christ denomination. In Coalson Interview 1/18, Charles speaks of his propitious attendance at an American Academy of Religion conference where a an unnamed Catholic nun at the gathering told him about CTS. At this time he wrote to the Dean at CTS, Professor Ron Osborn, and told him of his connection to William Robinson.

Yet within this cautious, ecumenical setting, Charles fought to keep his focus on his mission. He fought to stay on the path. He seemed to have a sense of who he was and what he was doing, where he was going. Charles was a mystical laborer, working for the pay that was due him, nothing more, nothing less. His expectations were not of this world, yet he was still a man, living in this world where good and evil were mixed together. Only those who had eyes to see could tell which was which.

Accepting the job at CTS was more than a professional move for Charles. It was a matter of friendship. In Coalson Interview 12/3, Charles says clearly that being at CTS was repaying Ronald Osborn and the Disciples. He knew that his life would be meaningful only when it was "other" centered. He says to Bob, "nothing is worse than self-centered people, they are prisoners of the gutter. Self-advancement is self-imprisonment." Charles saw it plainly; the British Protestants helped him recreate himself. He wanted to return the favor to the Protestants by living and working among them. With this in mind, he says to Bob (Interview 12/30) that he thought of himself as "a missionary of the party called civilization."

He often said that the everlasting genius of the existentialists was their contribution of the concept of decision-making. Even if the decision is a bad one, it is still better to have decided and moved on, rather than sit in limbo (Rev. 3:15-22). When one is uncertain, there results a draining of precious energy, which further confuses and destroys attention. Uncertainty is worse than a bad decision. Charles understood this concept and he applied it to his life at an early age, discernible to us (at least) by the time he was twenty-two. His decision to be an exile was not an intellectual decision. It was a decision of precision. This precision is from the science of the spirit which Jesus speak of in the Beatitudes in Matthew 5:2-12. Setting the mind on a course toward that which is pure and good remains more important than appearing pure and good in the eyes of family, country, church, friends. Pleasing God with purity of attention is more pressing than pleasing one's friends and family, the expectations of our upbringing, our education. Charles understood that no one is worthy of the Kingdom of Heaven if they put to the plow and turn back (Lk 9:62) Charles understood that the rich, young ruler was saddened by the answer Jesus gave him because he realized that his possessions were more than physical and monetary, that they came with a psychological price (Lk 18:18-25). There was a cosmic significance to the higher calling of God with eternal ramifications of being true to one's calling. His exile produced his calling, his role in the universe. To Charles, he was aware of his Montenegran blood and all its meaning. Yet he was also aware of the cosmic blood of Jesus Christ which he had discovered racing through his veins. This new blood caused his world to broaden from its provincial, Balkan gospel to a universal view, filled with unseen dimensions. He was working on this plane, this plane which speaks to the unseen yet lives in the seen. Charles knew his role in life and this conserved his energy. This conservation of energy allowed him to pay attention. To Charles, it was all about attention.

Behind Enemy Lines

In the summer of 1967, Charles again entered a strange, new landscape: the Bible Belt of America. Christianity in 1960's middle America was in the midst of the pseudo-revival of post World War Two. The predominant, white, middle class was prospering, while the African-American population was still fighting the largely unresolved issues of the American Civil War. America was at an ideological crossroads and Charles dropped right into the geographical crossroads of America--Indiana.

Charles brought with him a completely unacceptable American viewpoint; the disenfranchised immigrant. As an exile, Charles understood the disenfranchised immigrant. His life experience had helped shape his role in the building of the Kingdom of God. Charles understood what it was like to be without a country, to be without an identity. The experience of leaving behind one's known universe to the whims of unknown forces beckons legions of primordial fears. It opens the psyche to that collective source of eight thousand years of evolution of the human species where survival was the order of every moment. The danger of annihilation from the faceless force of nature is a seed that can quickly germinate and bear fruit in the human psyche, given the right combination of chaos and violence, isolation. Charles bore the fruit of such an experience. It was impossible for him to have experienced what he did at such a crucial period in his transition from youth to adult and not be affected in his outlook on the world. Indeed, his Serbian soil, coupled with the greenhouse effect of a devastating civil war and subsequent capitulation toward atheistic communists, altered the angle and shape of Charles' entire future. He now carried with him the outlook of a soldier in combat.

Old Testament Professor Dr. Gerry Janzen was a colleague of Charles' at CTS from 1968 to 1990. Dr. Janzen insightfully describes Charles as having been a "soldier dropped behind enemy lines." He fought covertly when needed and overtly when needed, with the realization that the battle was a matter of life and death. He fought with the knowledge that he had no support from any other troops. He related to the human world as being a matter of good versus evil, yet evil was not given the freedom to work alone. Good was on a mission, evil was on a mission and he was on a mission. His mission was clear to him and he sought out other human beings who were sympathetic to this humanistic cause. Many times those sympathizers he discovered did not even know they were sympathizers at the time. He was able to detect the faintest divine spark in another person and "alert" them to it before they even knew it was in existence. Yet he only pointed, he never willed someone in a certain direction.With those sympathizers to the cause, Charles had a "conspiratorial rapport," as Dr. Janzen describes it. There was a sense that the enemy was all about and secrecy needed to be kept. These secrets were known only to the children of Light, having been awakened in them through the fire of trials and sufferings. The children of Light recognize one another, tend to one another, sacrifice for one another, love one another as if their life depended upon it. This is the way Charles lived: as if his life depended upon his finding as many sympathizers to the cause as he could possibly manage, no matter what the cost was to himself.

The Legion

In order for a soldier to reach his potential, where his training equals his valor, he needs to have a cause in which to believe. This cause can lead him to fight on when the circumstances seem bleak and hopeless. This cause can strengthen the soldier's power of attention, giving him the advantage over the enemy. This cause can instill in the soldier a sense of sacrifice, so that their own well-being is not as important as the cause itself and those individuals who compose its main body.

The cause which Charles believed in was that of the redemption of the cosmos itself through the teaching and influence of Jesus of Nazareth. It was God's ability to speak the truly cosmic language of love through his birth, life, death and resurrection of Jesus Christ which attracted Charles to the cause. It was a cause of unity, calling on the world to decide to use it energy toward the goal of Being and Love, instead of controlling and consuming in a milieu of domination and destruction. The mark of true Christianity is when it guides a person along the road toward the proper use of freedom, toward unity, toward Being and Love. This means that true Christianity is profoundly interior. The cause which Christianity fights for is that of an individual human soul, on its journey to becoming a Spirit. This journey is lonely and long, a lifetime trial where the skills of inward listening are practiced and practiced.

Charles heard this call within his heart, this call for unity beckoned him. It was during his time of uncertainty and loneliness at the Praskvitza Monastery that he won a crucial victory in the struggle for being: he began to move from a knowledge of the cause of unity and love toward an understanding of the cause of unity and love. This was an interior struggle within his psyche at the same time his home and his homeland sank further into an uncertain and precarious future. His main enemy was lack of attention on this inward spark within him that had been fanned into a flame. He had to learn how to psychologically treat this with delicate attention. He was moving out into the unknown universe (around the Adriatic toward Italy) with literally nothing left but his attention. He was alone and needed allies. At this time he was given a surprisingly strong ally, one whom he would never meet face to face yet would come to know as an intimate friend--Fyodor Dostoevsky.

It is now time to hear in Charles' own words what has already been eluded to, namely the importance of Dostoevsky in the evolution of Charles Ashanin. In Dostoevsky, Charles found the preeminent psychologist of our time who was able to show him the struggle for Being which rages on within each human soul. Charles writes

> I read Dostoevsky with the devotion of a pupil for whom he provided illumination on all those problems of human life which tormented me. The chief of these was the problem of evil. Only those who have suffered and agonized as I did are able to

appreciate Dostoevsky. He takes one on the journey through all regions of the human soul and persistently guides one through its most fathomless depths and lays them bare to the searching of one's mind. It is a frightening but a fascinating adventure. But this journey is not for the sake of curiosity. Those who engage in it in this spirit are barred from going too far. And seeing this they give up the enterprise. But those who are motivated by a deep spiritual quest succeed because the spirit of human sympathy guides them on. There is no other way of describing what Dostoevsky has done for me except by saying that it was a sort of pilgrimage of which Dante in *The Divine Comedy* and John Bunyan in *Pilgrim's Progress* speak. It was both spiritually and psychologically a thorough therapeutic experience. Spiritually it helped me to exorcise many demons which through resentment of what I had been through had lodged themselves like leeches in the bottom of my being. And the only way of getting rid of them, Dostoevsky convinced me, was through forgiveness and love. For the first time in my life I understood the true meaning of Jesus' words: You have learned that they were told, 'love your neighbor, hate your enemy.' But what I tell you is this: love your enemies and pray for your persecutors; only so can you be children of your heavenly Father . . . " I used to think of these words as something bidden us to do for the sake of others, a sort of generosity on our part. But now I saw that this is far from being an act of benevolence for others; it is the only way by which we ourselves are freed from the chains of private demons which torture us from their fortress deep inside our own soul. There is no other way of dislodging them. But I soon discovered that to achieve this, man needs help. Dostoevsky reminded me also of another saying of Jesus that these fiends can only be got rid of through prayer and fasting. What frightened me was that I recognized that they were not one or two but an army of them--a legion living inside me. I realized also that my flight from the communists and their tyranny was useless as long as I was in bondage to the spiritual and psychological tyranny which dominated me from within. I was a walking civil war. My problem was that before anything else I had to restore peace in the domain of my own heart. [1]

Charles had made a crucial discovery and admission; the war for peace on any human level begins with an internal battle against the legion of selves which constitute a fallen, human existence. Charles refers to this in the previous passage as being the story from Luke 8:26-39. This is the passage where Jesus heals the Gerasene Demoniac. He approached this homeless, naked and physically tattered man living among the tombs. When he saw Jesus he begged him not to torment him. Jesus then asks a significantly ontological question, "What is your name?" in verse 30. [2] Throughout the Old and New Testament there seems to be a deep and theological significance in a name and in a renaming; Exodus 3:13-14, Genesis 32:27-30, Luke 6:14, Acts 9:1-9. It seems to be an identification by God of one who was lost, but now is on The Way. When God the Creator and a Created human being become aware of one another there results a change in both God and creature. God changes in that God receives back into Himself that element which had been lost. The human being changes by choosing to begin the process of becoming a true human being as God intended. We are not meant to remain divided internally yet masked over with the image of unity. We are meant to be a unified being, capable of the same love as Jesus Christ. Charles knew this fact, this law. While tending to the cows in the pasture of the Praskvitza Monastery, he began to understand this.

When Jesus asks the Demoniac "what is your name?", he says "Legion." When Charles was teaching at the University of Ghana, he wrote an essay first published in "The Greek Orthodox Theological Review" entitled *Images of God and Anti-God: Studies in the Metaphysics of Dostoyevski.* He writes,

> By way of estranged freedom man comes to know that inner division of self which is evil and demonic, for the separate parts of being become personified apart and engaged in each other's destruction. This is demonic possession-the presence of the demonic image in man and the world, the utter evil, the Devil. In *The Brothers Karamozov* Dostoyevski describes how Ivan Karamozov has fallen into this state of demonic division of being. He tells Satan: 'You are an incarnation of myself, but only one side of me--of my thoughts and feelings, and only of the nastiest stupidest of them . . . you are myself, but with a

> different face . . . you are not somebody else. You are I, and nothing more, you are my fancy.' In this cleavage we see the ugliness of non-being destroying being. He names it Sodom. [3]

In the notes to this essay, Charles cites a passage from one of his favorite philosophers, Nicholas Berdyaev.

> All Dostoevsky's "divided" people have a devil, though less clearly visible than Ivan's is to him. This second self is the spirit of not-being, it represents the loss of the essence of personality and is the manifestation of an empty liberty, the freedom of nothingness. The ideal of Sodom is only a ghost of life, and Svidrigailov, definitely given up to that ideal, himself becomes nothing more than a phantom with no vestige of personality left. Nothingness is immanent in evil. The divided man can find salvation nowhere but in the second, final, freedom, freedom in the grace and truth of Christ. To mend that inner cleavage and banish that nightmare of Satan a man must make a definitive choice, and choose Being itself. [4]

As has been previously stated, choice is a paramount issue. In Dostoevsky, Charles found a teacher who could *consistently* teach him in his *consistently* chaotic world. These early lessons in metaphysics and psychology laid the foundation for his entire life. It was this lesson regarding choice and freedom, good and evil, which began the key linkage between Charles' head and heart. Charles writes in his essay on Dostoevsky,

> How then, can man be saved from the attack of the demonic image?; through choice, personal choice for being. Dostoyevski gives all-important significance to this choice. And this explains why he contrasts the ugliness of Sodom, the final destruction of being, which is the metaphysical implication of the estranged freedom with the beauty of Our Lady, for in her wholehearted choice of God's will--"Let it be to me according to Your word"--lies the way towards God, towards unity with the community of being, where creative freedom united all things. [5]

The issue of choice implies freedom. Within the issue of freedom there is an implicit condition of "estranged freedom" and "creative freedom." For Charles, this bifurcation is a crucial point; God gives us the freedom to choose over non-being. There is no guarantee that the right choice will be made. Our psychological condition is so fragmented it takes a great amount of effort to continue to choose Being over Non-Being. Sometimes a life can be limited to playing roles. These roles are the embodiment of the "Legion" which Jesus identifies in Luke 8 and which Dostoevsky portrays as the different characters in his novels. His novels are essentially the story of the Legion within one human existence, what Charles calls "a planet peopled by denizens of its own." [6] In *The Brothers Karamozov* Dostoevsky writes, "But all his life, as a matter of fact, Fyodor Pavlovich was fond of playacting, of suddenly taking up some unexpected role right in front of you, often when there was no need for it, and even to his own real disadvantage . . . This trait, however, is characteristic of a great many people, even rather intelligent ones, and not only of Fyodor Pavlovich." [7]

Charles understood this; if he did not fight his own internal civil war, then his exile would be for nothing. He would simply be carrying his embattled and fragmented psyche with him wherever he went. He would have no peace unless he made a stand and fought for his true salvation, the salvation of his psyche. This ability to face your own demons, your own denizens is the height of human courage and dignity. It leaves the hero naked to all the threats and powers which are normally masked by the scattered mind. The true hero is anyone who uses this

God-graced freedom to fight for a square inch of peace within themselves. This fight, this zeal is for the cleansing of the mind of all the combatants, restoring the peace of God within the human soul and letting it spread throughout, transforming the soul into the Spirit. This is a true war, the unceasing struggle of a human lifetime to end the "walking civil war" which is all too often accepted as a normal existence. Charles understood what Jesus meant when he said "I have not come to bring peace, but the sword." (Mt 10:34) The sword is freedom and the arm that wields it is choice.

Notes on The Legion

1. Ashanin, Charles. "A Garland for a Mother." p 289-290.

2. Fyodor Dostoevsky's novel *The Possessed* is based on this passage from Luke 8:26-39.

3. Ashanin, Charles. *Essays on Orthodox Christianity and Church History*. p 191.

4. Berdyaev, Nicholas. "*Dostoevsky*" Meridian Books, New York, 1957, p 110.

5. Ashanin, *Essays*. p 191-192.

6. Ashanin, "Garland." p 1.

7. Dostoevsky, Fyodor. *The Brothers Karamozov,* Farrar, Straus and Giroux, New York, 1990, p 11.

Dostoevsky and Freedom

Here we must expound on the concept of freedom in the fiction of nineteenth century writer Fyodor Dostoevsky if we are to understand anything about the life of Charles Bozidar Ashanin. Charles understood Dostoevsky as saying humanity is in a fallen state of existence away from God, the Ultimate Being or Reality. In such a condition, humanity encounters God in and through the freedom within human existence. This freedom implies choice and this means that necessity is not the supreme motivator of our existence. In other words, this freedom allows us to have a choice outside of our primal, feral proclivity to dominate and control our environment. In this sense, God has infused God's Absolute freedom within creaturely freedom through the presence of Jesus the Cosmic Christ. By infusing this Absolute freedom within human existence, God takes an enormous risk. Human existence now has the knowledge of its estrangement from the Ultimate Reality and can choose to widen the gap by means of claiming existence as their own instead of honoring God as the source of freedom and existence. Freedom is infused into human existence in order to have a transformative effect, in essence it is the source of the energy that is needed to redeem humanity.

Freedom functions as a source of energy and is not therefore a final goal. The final goal is to have humanity transformed into a new creature. (Romans 8:18-25) Charles writes, "the intensity of the conflict is a tragedy which seeks redemption--the healing of the estrangement between Creator and creature--and the final triumph of freedom over necessity in man and the world." [1]

Charles understood Dostoevsky as seeing Christ (God-Man) as being the one who made the problem of Absolute freedom a human problem. Christ being man, took on the predicament of humanity's estrangement from God and infused within it the element of Absolute freedom, with its origins being cosmic and divine. Charles writes, "In Christ creaturely freedom meets Absolute freedom. In the Absolute freedom of God, revealed in Christ, creaturely freedom recognizes its transcendental source and its true nature. This creates in human existence a longing to overcome its fallen state, the cleavage and ruptures within existence." [2]

Within this human existence, freedom is recognized as being "bound up with personality." This means that freedom exposes the necessity dominated world as an illusion since it deprives freedom from existing. When necessity dominates, the world is denied becoming the beautiful creation of God, the Cosmos. Therefore creative freedom has a dual objective in its attempt to redeem humanity from its estrangement from God and also the restoring of the universe to its true nature. For Dostoevsky and Charles, this is the cosmic significance of the God-Man Jesus Christ. Through Christ and the revealed freedom, God, as "an absolutely free, unified and self-related reality . . . creates the being outside Himself and reveals His image in it. This means that He gives to His creation a *communal nature* because He is related to it in Love, that is, His creation is His own personal concern. Love is the inner drive of God towards creating being and infusing it with freedom. The presence of freedom in creation is the divine Providence upholding and guiding it." [3] Through Christ, freedom overcomes animal necessity and restores and maintains the new creature transformed by the Love of God, the Ultimate Reality and creator of the Cosmos.

Notes to Dostoevsky and Freedom

1. Ashanin, Charles. *Essays* p 185.

2. Ashanin, Charles. *Essays* p 186.

3. Ashanin, Charles. *Essays* p 185.

Image of God

In Dostoevsky, Charles began to understand the nuances between good and evil. Within his works, Dostoevsky contends that a human being is not an independent, singular creature. A human being, is in essence, a revelation of the images of God and anti-God within his or her personality. Within each creature, the divine and the demonic meet with each claiming the creature as its own.

In Vyacheslav Ivanov's classic work on Dostoevsky entitled *Dostoyevski: Freedom and the Tragic Life*, he writes of the two faces of Satan, namely Lucifer and Ahriman. Lucifer, the spirit of light which may be darkness (Luke 11:35) is the archetype of isolation. Ahriman, the spirit of the black abyss is the archetype of destruction. Both of these faces of evil owe their very existence upon the fact that they imitate true Being, yet they mutually negate one another in their sole purpose of attempting to destroy the image of God within man, like two empty mirrors facing one another. [1]

Charles saw clearly what Dostoevsky was pointing out that these two faces of evil had one source with one intention: through the world of illusion, the capturing, isolation and destruction of any evidence of the image of God within a human being. This action completes the destruction of the Soul within the creature. This world is bathed in illusion, subsequently wrong choices are made which have eternal ramifications. Creaturely freedom is mistaken for Divine, Absolute freedom. This creaturely freedom gives a human being the sense that the empirical world can be possessed, therefore anything is permitted. There are no rules in a world bathed in illusion. This gives the creature a brief sense of unity (that speck of time in between rising and falling), yet all that awaits is complete destruction of Being. Ivanov refers to this as St. John's "second death" in the book of Revelation.

Whereas the Spirit of Satan, with its two embodiments, seeks to isolate and destroy, the Spirit of the Divine seeks to unite the individual and the community of being. The Divine accomplishes this through its trinitarian structure. Through God's creative freedom, he seeks another to affirm his own being, not to oppose him. This seeking out is done in order that the other may exist and share in being. This seeking out and sharing of being is the creation of the community of being, which in turn allow for the sharing of God's love. [2] Charles regards Dostoevsky's portrayal of Father Zosima and Alyosha in *The Brothers Karamozov* as an ideal for this trinitarian structure where both renounce themselves and their selfhoods for the love of the other. This is God's personal principle of the community of being where this beauty of God's love will save the world from the isolation and destruction of Satan's goal of Non-Being. [3]

This search of the inner heart for true being can be elusive in this world bathed in illusion. Charles understood this. This illusion of being, the illusion of estranged freedom does not have an ontological source, rather it does have a metaphysical character. Charles saw something within the metaphysics of Dostoevsky that shot to his core: the Universal conflict within the empirical world between the conflicting images of God (Christ) and anti-God (anti-Christ). The battle ground is the human heart; salvation or destruction. The human heart can choose between the two kinds of freedom in order to distinguish between these images; creative or estranged freedom. Yet this choice is complicated by the fact that they both appear in Trinitarian form, as has already been eluded to. For Charles, this issue of discernment is a matter beyond importance. It is about being and non-being. He sees Dostoevsky's focus on the nuances of the trinitarian forms of God and anti-God as a great spiritual achievement. [4] By pointing out the ambiguities of form, man has the opportunity to be liberated from the hammer blows of form, transcending it in search of the essence within each human existence. This allows man the opportunity to unite with the Ultimate Reality, at the same time revealing the true, illusory nature of the trinitarian demonic structure. When this occurs then the human personality is free to choose its true transcendent nature in God and thus contribute (as a cell does in a healthy body) "toward bringing the Cosmic Conflict nearer to its final stage." [5]

Within this Cosmic Conflict there is a clue (suggested by the very exile of Charles Ashanin itself) regarding the issue of energy: the damning effect of stagnation. As Ivanov points out, the demonic forces can gain dominion over the human soul only at times of stagnation, when the human personality immerses itself in itself with such passions as anger, jealousy, fear, lust. [6] This self-determination rebels against God and His image within that heart, (or within society itself) stagnating, isolating and moving toward ultimate destruction and damnation. Man must remain active always distinguishing between the images of God and anti-God within himself. This activity naturally occurs within the purifying psyche of a human being as he or she strives toward that destined, nobler existence where human personality transcends form and merges with the Ultimate Reality to become a new creature, a new Christ.

Notes on Image of God

1. Ivanov, Vyachelsav. *Dostoevsky: Freedom and the Tragic Life.* The Noonday

Press, New York, 1957, p 120.

2. Ashanin, Charles. *Essays.* p 188.

3. Ashanin, Charles. *Essays.* p 190.

4. Ashanin, Charles. *Essays.* p 187.

5. Ashanin, Charles. *Essays.* p 187.

6. Ivanov. p 130.

The Industry of the Pit

As each individual human being is a Legion unto itself, both singular and plural at the same time, so too is a society when it becomes a "multiplicity of depersonalized individuals, bound by no universal oneness in Love." [1] The relationship between individual and society is organic in nature, just as cells collectively constitute a single human body. When one cells begins to divide and multiply upon itself, this threatens the whole existence of the organism. The organism cannot sustain even one cell which acts beyond the boundary of its created purpose. This multiplicity spreads, creating death where once there was life.

Both cell and organism have a destined purpose, an intentional existence that is organically linked to one another. The organism remains dependent upon the cells to remain true to their designed purpose, so that it too can realize its designed purpose. The issue of Legion within a single individual is therefore an issue for society as well. When the sickness of Legion spreads within a human being, it seeks other prey when the meat is picked off the bone. The appetite, insatiable, to isolate and destroy, apprehend and dominate, will gain its artificial energy anywhere and anyhow. The Spirit of Legion seeks out. It is never idle. It never stagnates. Without an awareness of this potent appetite, the spirit can enter a human being almost undetected and immediately claim this divine territory as its own. When this "pax Legion" gains enough psychic ground within enough human beings within a given society then that society in effect becomes a collective Legion, a decaying pile of "dead souls, the dust storm of hell." [2]

A society such as this cannot hope to survive for any length of time, for any quality of existence. No amount of a religion which simply imitates a given morality can save a civilization which turns in upon itself and begins to devour its own, becoming a Lucifer and Ahriman industry of isolation and destruction. A healthy civilization depends upon the psychological health of its members. That civilization, in turn, promotes the perpetuation of the established role model of psychological health for its members. This allows for a norm to be established within a civilization, with its members held accountable toward a certain development, an emotional maturity. This is education beyond the intellect. This is education of the heart where a human being's emotional center is developed and this issue of Legion is addressed (Matt 10:34). A civilization which only addresses the education of its members on the levels of intellect and motor skills is a ship without a rudder. It floats, it sails, yet it is stripped of its ability to hold a course, left powerless to the rule of current and wind. A destination may be in mind, but stronger currents take over.

A civilization must work while it is daylight (Mk 13:32-36) to educate its members so that they may discover their individual purpose and eternal destiny. This singularity allows for this range of motion while continuing to be engaged with the same laws which have the potential to dominate purpose and eradicate independence. The Gospel of Saint Matthew describes this in the stories of Jesus calming the storm in 8:23-27 and Jesus walking on the water in 14:22-33. In both stories, Jesus represents this singularity who overcomes the stronger laws. The stronger laws are not eradicated, yet they are slowed down and viewed from a different perspective. This allows for freedom of movement and conservation of energy. Stagnation and direction. Legion and singularity. Death and life.

When a civilization contains members who are moving from Legion to singularity, that civilization in turn begins to galvanize into a singularity, moving with purpose, independence. It then begins to function as an instrument of Light. Its policies toward its own and its relationship with other civilizations has direction and meaning: the fostering of life by society. Its policies rise and are implemented by a desire to see each member fulfill their designed destiny. Personalities are encouraged to meet their potential, both on the individual and societal scales. In this singularity, unity is discovered.

Notes on The Industry of the Pit

1. Ivanov. p 140.

2. Ivanov. p 141.

His Role As An Ecumenic: Part 1

Any true understanding of the ecumenical unity within the Cosmic Christ bases itself on the progress toward singularity, on both the individual and social spectrum. This is a process, a movement from Legion to singularity which is not an isolated act of becoming. Rather, it is a lifelong task of re-educating the soul, training it to become a Spirit with the trait of permanent love. Therefore, the ecumenical movement within and among all three branches of Christianity during the twentieth century arose out of a desire to work toward unity. Ivanov writes,

> The ecumenical oneness of all in Christ . . . is a union in which the uniting personalities achieve a complete development and a clear outlining of their peculiar and original entities of their integral creative freedom. In each of them the Word has found its embodiment. It dwells in all, and from each it is heard in a different and special fashion. Yet the Word in the utterance of each is echoed in

> all; and all are the one free unity, for all are the One Word. [1]

Charles Ashanin was an ecumenic through and through. His life, his destiny as a child of Light was realized because of his contact with other Christians on a global, non-provincial scale who saw Christian unity as not simply an issue within church polity or two-dimensional theology. Charles saw the ecumenical issue as one of stagnation and direction, legion and singularity, death and life. To a true ecumenic the cosmic future of the Christian religion is dependent upon the movement toward a common knowledge, understanding and experience of the same triune God. Charles was plucked from the fire by men of such belief and never forgot the eschatological nature of such a sacrifice. In a 1991 letter to Dr. Paul A. Crow, Jr., Charles writes,

> I am and have always been an Orthodox among you for one reason only, because people like you are my fellow Christians whom I do not see as being spiritually different from myself. I reciprocate your sentiments fully and I want you to know that just an nothing can separate us from the love of God, nothing will weaken my love in Christ for

you, for long ago it has acquired an eschatological character. [2]

Notes to His Role as an Ecumenic: Part 1

1. Ivanov. p 141.
2. Ashanin, Charles, unpublished letter to Dr. Paul A. Crow, Jr., Jan 14, 1991.

Interlude: Florovsky

In the summer of 1964, Charles, Natalie, Lydia and Marina left Columbia, South Carolina and moved to Cambridge, Massachusetts. Charles had been accepted as a Lilly Postdoctoral Fellow at Harvard Divinity School (1964-65). In the summer of 1964, Georges Florovsky retired from Harvard Divinity School, where he had been teaching Church History (Patristics, Christian Spirituality and Liturgics) since 1956. The lives and theologies of Charles Ashanin and Georges Florovsky parallel in striking ways.

Florovsky was born in 1893 in Russia. He was an acclaimed Russian Orthodox intellectual and priest who after completing his academic training at the University of Odessa, was accepted as a part of the faculty in 1919. However, by 1920 the political and social situation within the Soviet Union had become so precarious that he and his family immigrated to Sofia, Bulgaria and soon afterwards to Prague, Czechoslovakia. [1] He received his Ph.D. in 1923 from the Russian University Center in Czechoslovakia, where he soon began teaching. He joined the St.

Sergius Institute in 1926 in Paris where it became the center of Russian Orthodoxy in Western Europe. St. Sergius became a very influential presence in the flowering ecumenical movement in the West by training priests, teachers and lay leaders. It was at St. Sergius that Florovsky found his true vocation--Patristics. He found that the Early Church Fathers were beacons to a better understanding of the culture of Russia, Greece and England. But he also discovered that the Early Church Fathers provided a foundation for the flowering ecumenical movement.

One of the ways however, in which Charles and Florovsky differed was in the fact that Florovsky was an ordained Orthodox priest (1932), whereas Charles felt compelled to remain a layman. Charles always felt completely comfortable in his role in the Orthodox Church. Charles and Florovsky were similar in their personal contact and influence by the English and the Scottish. Florovsky had contact with them through the Fellowship of St. Allen and St. Sergius. From 1929 until the war he was invited by Nicholas Zernov to speak at the Fellowship's annual conference which mainly met in England. These Anglican-Orthodox conferences allowed Florovsky to move into the English-speaking Western culture of England, where he soon felt at home.

His British contacts outside the Orthodox world brought him into contact with the rising ecumenical movement. He attended the historic Second Conference on Faith and Order in Edinburgh, Scotland in August of 1937 where he was one of seven chosen to organize the World Council of Churches. This was the apex of the ecumenical movement with an Orthodox as one of its main authors. [2]

Another connection between Charles and Florovsky was that Florovsky and his wife lived in Yugoslavia from 1941 to 1944. He taught at a high school for boys called the Russian Cadet Corps, which was located east of Belgrade. By the summer of 1944 the Axis Powers began to give way to the Partisans and this prompted the Florovsky's to move north to Czechoslovakia and back to Paris by December of 1945. [3] By September of 1948 the Florovsky's moved to New York City where he became Professor of Dogmatic Theology and Patristics at St. Vladimir's Orthodox Seminary and Dean by 1949. It was here that he began to find his Orthodox voice in the ecumenical movement. In Andrew Blane's major essay on the life of Georges Florovsky, he writes that "Florovsky's chief objective as the new Dean was to give St. Vladimir's Seminary a pan-Orthodox, ecumenical orientation. This meant in the new American context disengaging the Orthodox populace from a 'preoccupation with ethnic nostalgias . . . and inherited animosities' and rooting the Orthodox faith into the life of their adopted homeland. It was a struggle not only with habits from the past, but the taste for the past. Many in the Church resisted efforts to indigenize Orthodoxy into the new world, instinctively identifying the native and the national which they sought to preserve as both Orthodox and true." [4]

Florovsky was intent on tacking a new course for American/Western Orthodoxy in a post-World War II world. He saw the task of the contemporary Orthodox theologian as essentially addressing an ecumenical audience, since to him Orthodoxy is not provincial in its essence, but ecumenical. [5] He was greatly concerned by the proclivity of the Orthodox in America to sink down into old nationalistic traditions and identities, thereby shunning their newly adopted homeland. In a landmark speech to the twenty-third annual National Convention of the Federation of Russian Orthodox Clubs in Philadelphia in September of 1949, Florovsky says, " . . . we are consistently tempted to reduce our Orthodoxy to our nationality. Now, Christianity is a universal truth . . . It is not a delicate thing which must be protected. Christianity is a weapon which is given to men to be used in a resolute fight with evil and for truth on earth . . . "

[6] To Florovsky, the task of Orthodoxy (as the bearers of the "true Church") was the same as the ecumenical movement: UNITY. Yet there was a distinctive and vital difference (as Florovsky and Charles Ashanin discovered) between the involvement in the ecumenical movement by the Orthodox and the ecumenical movement in American Protestant Christianity. That difference was *eschatology*. To the Orthodox, as Florovsky expressed it, the ecumenical movement was not one born out of the caldron of Dantean, Twentieth Century geopolitics. Rather, it was a continuation of the original message of the Galilean master, namely a call for unity in the Holy Spirit for all of humanity. There is an aphorism by Robin Amis:

> The hunger for God is a hunger for unity.
>
> This hunger begins to be satisfied in unity with others.
>
> When we are without forgiveness, we are without unity,
>
> So it follows that we are forgiven only when we forgive.
>
> Unity with God is unity with everyone.

This unity within the body of Christ was the driving force behind Florovsky's involvement within the ecumenical movement itself. He expressed his deep concern about the problem of disunity at the Second Assembly of the World Council of Churches at Evanston, Illinois in August of 1954. Within its first decade of existence, the World Council of Churches began to shift its emphasis from the problem of disunity toward the attempt to solve the global material and social problems.

This call for unity within the body of Christ was not merely a deontological expression of ethics. It was teleological in nature because it was eschatological. To Florovsky, the goals of the true, unifying, ecumenical movement had Christ as its hope for the world. To people like Florovsky and Karl Barth, hope is an eschatological category. [7] This hope was for the unity within the body of Christ that would witness the coming of the Kingdom of God on Earth: the end, the last, the extreme. This was the long awaited victory of good over evil, insuring truth on earth. The preparation for the coming of this truth is not accomplished simply by the solving of economic and social problems of the world. To Florovsky and the Orthodox witness within the first decade of the World Council of Churches, the problem was not the political and economic issues of social justice. The problem was disunity within Christianity itself. The Body needed to heal and become whole.

Notes to Interlude: Florovsky

1. Florovsky, Georges. *Georges Florovsky: Russian Intellectual, Orthodox Churchman*. Edited by Andrew Blane. St. Vladimir's Seminary Press. Crestwood, NY 10707. 1993. p 33,42.
2. Florovsky. p 72-74.
3. Florovsky. p 81.
4. Florovsky. p 94.
5. Florovsky. p 92.
6. Florovsky. p 93.
7. Florovsky. p 107.

His Role As An Ecumenic: Part 2

The ecumenical spirit which Charles had throughout his life in the West was forged by men with the same philosophy as Georges Florovsky. There was an eschatological character to the ecumenical camaraderie which Charles experienced in such men as Dr. Charles Raven and Dr. Nicholas Zernov. Charles saw that this Englishman and Russian both had the same goal in mind: the unity of the body of Christ. Charles' ecumenical philosophy was affected by his experiences during the war. It caused him to see the world in a different way. In America, he saw himself as a soldier fighting behind enemy lines. It was in England and Scotland where he underwent his training in the art of spiritual warfare.

After arriving in England with the help of men like Charles Raven, he learned from men like Nicholas Zernov that an Eastern Orthodox Montenegran could survive in Western society. But Charles needed a mentor. He found this mentor in

William Robinson. In his introduction to Charles' book of essays, Dr. Osborn quotes a portion of a 1989 letter from Charles,

> Those preparing for His service as you and I did had no choice but to study Christian religion ecumenically which in my case was in England, at Selly Oak Colleges, where my first ecumenical mentor was William Robinson, and afterwards in Scotland, at Glasgow University, from 1949-55. [1]

Dr. Robinson was the first western theologian who taught Charles about the Protestant tradition in the West. He was the Principal of Overdale College, which was maintained by the Churches of Christ (closely related to the Disciples of Christ in the United States).

Dr. Robinson was a leading theologian in the ecumenical movement which pervaded his teaching and his life's work. He soon left Overdale for the United States to become the chair of the School of Religion at Butler University, which had been founded in 1924. By 1958, Butler's School of Religion became an independent institution under the name of Christian Theological Seminary.

As Charles became acquainted with the twin histories of the Christian West and East, he became convinced of the galvanizing impact of the indwelling Spirit of Christ upon all of human history. Charles was one of the rare examples of someone willing to stand with one foot in the past and one foot in the future. This enabled him to see beyond the provincial nature of much of Orthodoxy in the postwar West and beyond the myopic only-child syndrome of Protestantism in America. This ability prepared him nobly for the task ahead.

His experiences immediately following his earning a Ph.D. in 1955 were rich in ecumenical diversity with a five-year stay in Western Africa at the University of Ghana. He then spent seven years at two different African Methodist Episcopal Colleges in South Carolina during the awakening of justice in 1960's American South. The culmination of his ecumenical journey began with the position of Associate Professor in Early Church History at Christian Theological Seminary in Indianapolis, Indiana. The key to his presence in Indiana was ecumenical.

It is the belief of this biographer that the seminal nature of his ecumenical existence is founded in his early childhood. In an act of faith and keen insight, his grandfather and his parents realized that he had gifts beyond what provincial Iskoci, Montenegro could offer in 1920. He was introduced to a world outside his family at an early age, especially with his training at Secondary School. By going to great lengths, his parents gave his personality permission to seek beyond them, to explore outside the boundary of family and search through the means of education for an as yet unspoken sense of wholeness. It was this act of humanistic love which matched circumstances with personality in young Bozidar. This freedom was a perfect ingredient in his life. He had a familiarity with an unknown which wanted to be known. For Charles, an ecumenic was also an epistemologist.

This epistemological spirit began to take on ecumenical characteristics in Charles as the Second World War crudely collided with the Civil War in Yugoslavia between the Chetniks and the Partisans. Charles had the seeds of a wider, multidimensional universe sown within him at an early age. The confrontational nature of the war sparked with his personality was the fire storm that raged through his soul, burning and consuming, altering the landscape of his interior life. What remained was a new land, initially barren and stark. Yet God abhors a vacuum, and dormant seeds that lay on the forest floor for years were now cracked open by the intensity of the conflagration. New and rare trees sprouted in this lunaresque landscape, the soil rich and black, chthonian figures loomed behind stumps and charred giants. Charles lived with an illumination from the sun, yet also with a hyper-alertness from the shadows it created--stagnation and direction, legion and singularity, death and life.

The arrival of the Ashanin's in Indianapolis, Indiana also witnessed the arrival of their third child, Valerie. This Midwestern town was to be the last home for the Ashanin's as they chose to raise their family in this agrarian environment known for its hospitality and sports. In 1967, Christian Theological Seminary was nine years old, having just recently become an independent entity out of nearby Butler University in the geographic center of Indianapolis. Without a doubt, Charles was made familiar with the very existence of CTS due to the mentoring of William Robinson. Another influence which drew him toward the Hoosier state (with its southern half influenced greatly by Scotch-Irish immigrants) was the presence of J. Irwin Miller in nearby Columbus, Indiana. Although Miller was an industrialist by profession, he was a leading ecumenist of his day, serving as the president of the National Council of Churches from 1960-63, as well as a member of the executive committee of the Central Committee of the World Council of Churches from 1961-68. In a letter dated June 24, 1968, Charles wrote to Mrs. Robert Tangeman, J. Irwin Miller's sister. She was a member of the board of trustees at CTS when Charles was hired in 1967. His letter shared with her his installation address and also expressed his deep sentiment toward her brother. He writes, "my decision to come to Christian Theological Seminary was partly influenced by the connection of your brother, Irwin, with it. It was a part of my Christian loyalty to him after his celebrated debate in the South two years ago with Fulton Lewis Jr., organized by a group of anti-National Council of Church Christians . . . Never before has anyone in our generation defended the prophetic tradition of our religion with concern for man as a creature of God as your brother did. When you see him please tell him of this." [3]

The milieu at Christian Theological Seminary at the time he was hired was steeped with ecumenical excitement. Even though it was a separate entity (since 1958) created and financed through the support of the Disciples of Christ denomination, the school had already begun to gather an impressive ecumenical core of students with twenty-six different communions present. [4] There was the feeling that CTS was at a turning point in its own history, as well as a turning point in the history of Christianity itself and the church universal. This was to be the Christian Century and CTS wanted to be a part of it. This desire to be a part of the unifying nature of the ecumenical movement began to take shape in the form of hiring well-trained faculty from not only a myriad of denominational backgrounds within Protestantism itself, but also from different traditions within Christianity itself. CTS also sought to strengthen ties with Jewish and Roman Catholic traditions. In short, CTS was looking to broaden its academic scope, offering a less myopic view for its students who were being trained and sent out into this new landscape. Obtaining an ecumenically-minded, Orthodox scholar from Eastern Europe with an already rich portfolio of academic experiences from Selly Oaks to Glasgow to Geneva to Ghana to Princeton to Harvard to South Carolina was an academic coup for young Christian Theological. Charles filled an urgent and exciting need for this young seminary. This seminary also filled a need for Charles and his family. It gave them ground, ground to grow as individuals and as a family.

The mindset needed at this academic institution to hire an Orthodox was due in some key measure to the influence of Dr. Frank J. Albert. He was the Professor of Early Church History and Thought at CTS until his death in 1965. According to Dr. Ronald Osborn, Dr. Albert, himself a member of the Disciples of Christ, said, "I did not cease to be an Orthodox when I became a Disciple." [5] As did Charles in his twenty-three years at CTS, Dr. Albert was to a large degree the unofficial chaplain for the seminary. There may have been official chaplains appointed by the Seminary, yet Dr. Albert and Charles were the men students gravitated toward when they needed guidance and consolation. Dr. Albert had set an important academic and social tone in the life of the seminary which made the hiring of Charles Ashanin seem to be a progressive and natural act.

Notes to His Role as an Ecumenic: Part 2

1. Osborn, Dr. Ronald, Introduction to *Essays in Orthodox Christianity and Church History* by Charles Ashanin. p 7.

2. Ashanin, Charles. Unpublished letter to Rev. William Baker, April 26, 1973.

3. Ashanin, Charles. Unpublished letter to Mrs. Robert Tangeman, June 24, 1968.

4. Osborn, Dr. Ron. Introduction to *Essays*, p 8.

5. Osborn, Dr. Ron. Introduction to *Essays*, p 9.

Part III

Cosmos

The Second Front

"Hey you. We used to send missionaries to people like you."-- remark to Charles from a CTS colleague (court records, p 72.)

On July 26, 1993 the United States District Court in Indianapolis, Indiana heard oral testimony of a civil law suit filed by plaintiff Charles B. Ashanin against defendant Christian Theological Seminary. The suit against his employer of twenty-three years charged that CTS discriminated against him because of his religious beliefs as an Eastern Orthodox Christian. He was seeking compensation for wages from November 1971 (the date of his being awarded tenure status at CTS) until December of 1990 that were lower than other tenured professors.

In the deposition to cause number IP 93-196 C, the defendant is asked to give proof of discrimination. In his testimony he gives several incidents as evidence, one of those being a faculty retreat to French Lick, Indiana in 1979. At this retreat the faculty were divided into pairs and asked to reevaluate the curriculum at CTS. Each pair was given a different subject for reassessment. Charles was paired with no one and given the assignment of preparing a statement on the organization of theological education within Eastern Orthodoxy. Each presentation was critiqued. The evaluator of Charles' assignment was direct. On the witness stand, Charles remembered the incident,

> He was man of great authority psychologically dominating all those people around him in his presence . . . but authoritarianism is alien to me, I have to tell you. I have to tell you this and he said, "Well, I am Protestant . . . you are an eastern Orthodox . . ." He said, "I as a Protestant I live in the modern world."
>
> Well, I was little bit embarrassed because I thought I lived in the modern world and, but my presence in the modern world I felt was negated because of this backward looking form, primitive form of faith I came from and he said, "You are an Orthodox. You live in the past. You have nothing to teach us," and he sat down . . .

> I said that experience at French Lick . . . was a devastating experience for me and if I had means– my options were limited to move somewhere else. I was getting older. I had a family; but if I had means to move from that environment in which I was humiliated I would. I would have left that place because I felt that I was no longer included in that community. [2]

During the retreat Charles shared a room with a certain fellow professor. After the hammer blows dealt by the humiliating evaluation, the professor remarked to Charles, "Certain people never got reconstructed." [3] In the deposition Charles states that at first he was consoled by these remarks in that the evaluator was a Protestant who "lived in a sectarian world and, these new ecumenical things did not reach him." [5] Charles later asked this certain professor, with whom he had shared the room at French Lick, to clarify his remarks and he clearly indicated to Charles that he was referring to him and not the evaluator as someone not willing or able to evolve theologically and spiritually.

In the deposition, Charles refers to another certain professor in an incident shortly after the 1979 French Lick retreat made the following statement:

> He said to me, looked at his watch... He said, "Ecumenical era at CTS is over." That meant, sir, that, the interpretation I got, that I was appointed at Christian Theological Seminary not because I was a scholar but because in his interpretation Christian Theological Seminary was some kind of ecumenical zoo in which people from various traditions were brought together for some... whatever reason and I felt that that statement was due to the very thing that we are talking about, that my tradition did not really have any impact. [6]

In the last major piece of evidence presented by the plaintiff during oral examinations, Charles referred to a incident in the early 1980's of plagiarism by a student. Charles discovered that a student had blatantly plagiarized a paper in one of his courses. Charles consulted two certain professors about the claim, and they agreed that it was a case of plagiarism. Charles then informed the student that another paper needed to be submitted. The student consulted an advisor who recommended that the student bring the issue to the attention of the Administration.

Charles believed he was not in a personal battle with this certain student or with the seminary itself. Charles felt that this was an issue of ethics for the seminary. He felt that he was protecting the seminary. [7] The administration gave their full support to the student. Charles was pressed to admit that he was wrong in his accusation of the student. Charles would not admit that he was wrong, even under implicit threat of termination of his employment at CTS. [8] The Administration finally had the paper graded, and a letter of exoneration was given to the student.

In Coalson Interview 12/3, Charles spoke of the threatening environment in which he lived during his escape from execution by the Communists as a time of tangible fear. He says that when his life was threatened, his first instinct was to retract within himself, into an actual self-imprisonment. Yet Charles believed that God allowed him to not withdraw into himself. He said, "I am a coward, not a courageous person . . . " but he learned ". . . to be a person who lived not to be afraid." He remarked that he learned to keep fear at bay. Otherwise he would have betrayed God's gift of freedom. For Charles, it came down to the proper use of the freedom which God gave him. He would not allow anyone to define him, otherwise it meant idolatry. He says,

> Don't give into fear, otherwise you give into the demonic . . . Keep fear at arms length. If we give into fear, we allow demonic forces to control us, and if we do that we disengage from our liberator Savior and become slaves of the force that is trying to corrupt this garden of flowers that Jesus has planted for us to give us consolation.

For Charles the element of intimidation and conflict had higher meanings, cosmic meanings. His struggle rose above the conflicts of personalities.

Notes to The Second Front

1. Ashanin, Charles, unpublished journal to Valerie Ashanin Abshire, p 31.

2. U.S. District Court, Southern District of Indiana, Indianapolis Division cause number IP 93-196 C; Associated Reporting, Inc., Two Market Square Center, 251 East Ohio Street, Suite 940, Indpls., IN 46204. July 26, 1993, p 58-59, 62-63.

3. Court Records. p 63.

4. Osborn, Dr. Ronald, Introduction to *Essays*, p

9.

5. Court Records. p 64.

6. Court Records. p 68.

7. Ashanin, Charles. Valerie's Journal, p 23.

8. Ashanin, Charles. Valerie's Journal, p 23-24. 3.

"Noli Me Tangere"

"I want to enunciate, talk about... You see, I could write about these things, but Bob, the living speech is much more significant, it is living, it is something shared instead of buried in, although this will be buried in the silence of time once it has been spoken or shared by two of us in the presence of angels so things we have spoken to each as human beings, this is recorded by...on another plane so that it has a certain element of transcendence about it."

-- Coalson Interview 2/17, two weeks before his death.

The author interviewed three former colleagues who worked alongside Charles during his tenure at CTS. Dr. Ed Towne and Dr. Gerry Janzen were professors of Theology and Old Testament respectively. Dr. Dick Dickinson was Dean of CTS for twelve years and President for ten years. Their reflections on Charles suggest a distant and complex colleague. Initially, Charles was a "congenial" and "positive" staff member. Yet it seems that

Charles never grew close to any colleagues. Dr. Towne remembered his conversations with Charles as always being one-sided. He never let the focus remain on himself. By the way in which he interacted with others on staff, it is clear that Charles felt isolated from others and never seemed to draw close to any of them. Dr. Janzen has already been quoted as describing Charles' relationship with others as searching for those other "soldiers." This conspiratorial rapport took its toll in the academic environment at CTS.

Charles was hired by the administration at CTS in the spirit of ecumenism. Yet shortly after his hiring and the awarding of tenure, that window closed abruptly. In a brief amount of time he had become an ecumenical anomaly within a social justice milieu of a liberal, Protestant seminary in the Bible Belt of America. His isolation, the exile itself, continued at CTS. The pangs were more pronounced now. A physical home was illusory to him. His true home had an inward and private distinction. This sense of isolation and inwardness was easily misinterpreted as an aloofness and a backwardness resulting from a primitive, out-of-date branch of the church with a quaint and eccentric exile from Montenegro as its sole representative.

Dr. Dickinson described Charles as someone who stayed at home theologically, therefore was unable to understand the structure of Western Civilization. This refusal to adapt to his new environment mixed roughly with a perceived conflict with the hierarchical structure of an academic institution. Dr. Dickinson described Charles as a poor teacher who consistently received negative yearly evaluations for lack of publications, lack of participation on committees and a general lack of quality in his teaching style. [1] These poor evaluations resulted in no yearly cost-of-living increases which was the reason for his comparatively low salary and his subsequent law suit in civil court. The civil law suit occurred during Dr. Dickinson's tenure as President of C.T.S. To Dr. Dickinson, Charles was stuck in Eastern Europe and unable to think outside the box of Orthodoxy, the foundation to his Serbian upbringing. Furthermore, Dr. Dickinson asserted that Charles' claims of a lack of appreciation for Orthodoxy only masked his sensitivity and defensiveness over a possible underlying sense of guilt from leaving his homeland and betraying his people. This guilt, to Dr. Dickinson, was the possible source of Charles' "fragile psyche." Subsequently, Charles misread his roles as a professor in a Western, academic environment. Said Dr. Dickinson, Charles was "too sensitive for his own good."

Dr. Janzen described Charles neurologically and psychologically in that he had a hyper-alertness stemming from the death at age five of his twin brother. Dr. Janzen's wife Eileen said that "only half of him survived." Dr. Janzen stated that Charles had two levels to him. The first level was that of a Christian Humanist/Cosmopolitan. The second level was the insider/outsider concept of the Balkan psyche with a good versus evil outlook on reality. Dr. Janzen remarked that Charles "exuded Eastern Orthodox Spirituality." He was "profoundly interior" with the ability to sense another human beings psychological toxicity. Dr. Janzen remembered several times of approaching Charles in the halls at CTS and before any handshake could take place, Charles would say "Noli Me Tangere." This is Latin for "Don't touch me."

This "Noli Me Tangere" was interpreted by the administration at CTS as a de-evolution. There was a sense that Charles was continuing to relive his exile and was consistently unable to adapt to his new environment. This new academic environment was based loosely on Process, Post-Holocaust and Liberation Theology, which quickly took root. According to Dr. Towne, there was a general pattern at CTS of respecting those people who made waves from the outside, but not from the inside. As Dr. Janzen remarked, systems have mechanisms for self-preservation.

This self-preservation may or may not be based on deception and illusion. Systems such as an academic institution, religious denominations or a democracy can be fixated on self-preservation to the point that original goals are obscured or even lost. When a system loses its goal, the demonic begins to reveal its measure of influence, initially by isolating the system. This isolation strengthens the deception and illusion. It is a decapitation, of sorts. The system then begins the process of feeding upon itself. This feeding on its own flesh is a slow act of destruction, annihilation. The demonic convinces a legion (in the form of a person, a corporation or a nation) that it is self-sustainable, in need of no other sustenance, no other food than its own flesh. It believes this, marvels at it, basks in its revelatory light. The blind happily lead the blind down a well lit, rocky path, everyone convinced that their survival is destined. When a human being identifies himself with a system, that system consumes them.

Charles was well acquainted with systems that were in the process of self-preservation. Firstly, he confronted the family/tribal system of his clan and country. It is this system which Jesus refers to in Mark 10:29-31 when he says,

> Truly I tell you, there is no one who has left house or brothers or sisters or mother or father or children or fields, for my sake and for the sake of the good news, who will not receive a hundred fold now in this age--houses, brothers and sisters, mothers and children, and fields with persecutions--and in the age to come eternal life. But many who are first will be last, and the last will be first. (NRSV)

Charles was relentless and steady in this respect throughout his life as a son, brother, a husband and a father. His primary loyalty was not to family of flesh and blood. His primary loyalty was to the family of the Spirit of God.

Secondly, he confronted the system of the outer church and its own proclivity to obscure and oftentimes deny the existence of the inner church. Charles was not given to the tribal nature of Western-based Orthodoxy, nor was he given to the bureaucratic politics of the Serbian Orthodox Church in Montenegro at the time of his exile. Charles knew the distinctive qualities of the outer and the inner churches. He saw the importance of the outer church as being the entry way to the inner church, the inner life. However, there is a boundary and it must be maintained. John speaks of this in his Gospel when he writes, "The one who comes from above is above all; the one who is of the earth belongs to the earth and speaks about earthly things. The one who comes from heaven is above all. He testifies to what he has seen and heard, yet no one accepts his testimony. Whoever has accepted his testimony has certified this, that God is true. He whom God has sent speaks the words of God, for he gives the Spirit without measure. The Father loves the Son and has placed all things in his hands. Whoever believes in the Son has eternal life; whoever disobeys the Son will not see life, but will endure God's wrath." (John 3:31-36 NRSV)

Charles knew and understood the importance of the division between, and the combining and the repetition of, the outer and inner churches. They are variables within an equation, working together to bring about a correct sum. When correctly identified and combined, they automatically bring about the sum. This answer never changes. It is eternal.

In a conversation with the author, Charles once said, "Arrogance is good because it keeps people from taking you over, taking advantage of you. Don't let anyone define you. If you do, it is idolatry." Charles was thoroughly aware of this distinction within himself. Within him there was a geography which had landscapes with breadth and width and height which knew no limits. Within him there was the presence of the Resurrected Christ. With this presence there was the overwhelming reality of the overcoming of the limitations of matter and time. Through this Christ's presence within Charles, the decaying element of time was abolished. Through this Christ's presence within Charles, the isolating element of matter was abolished. In one concise and precise motion, the resurrection destroys the effects of Satan; that of Lucifer in his isolation and Ahriman in his destruction. The victory of Christ is one which addresses the key human predicament--the economy of the return to God. This is Christianity, *the Way,* as it addresses our lostness and the difficulty in finding our way back to God.

This difficulty is primarily due to the fact that this world is a mixture of good and evil. It ever remains the arduous task of the prodigal child to use discernment in discovering what is good and discovering what is evil. Charles understood this arduous task all too well. He understood it in terms of *gnoseology*, or the interrelationships between personalities. He saw his life as a human being as one which was based on friendship. This friendship was not based loosely on the boundaries of social relationships. Rather this friendship was based on the *Christique* element within each person, which says that this kind of friendship is rooted in a loyalty to the other self, the other ego.

The love between two Christian friends is a love which has the power to overcome separation. In Charles' eyes, love is a power which unites. Therefore, it is an active power.

Separation is a passive element and can be overcome. The Christ within Charles had reached this active stage, this resurrected stage. The Christ within Charles now actively sought out its own self, its own nature, that particle of its own being that lay dormant within the psyche of every human being. This was the "conspiratorial rapport," the soldier behind enemy lines searching for allies.

His friendships were based on this common element of Christ within the other. Charles was not initially interested in the personality as a basis for friendship, although gnoseologically this was a key element in the relationship. Charles was not interested in socially pleasing others. He was interested in calling out your Christ from the depth of the tomb. He was interested in the Christ within you being awakened. His friendship was based not in social mores, but within a philosophy of humanity which addressed a divine nature within that other person.

Therefore, Charles was militant in his protection of his Christ, his internal, resurrected Christ. Its mission was his mission: Search for its own nature within humanity. This protection was a major goal. To him, if his main concern was another person's illusory feeling of security, then he was moving in the direction of identification. He would not allow himself to be identified with another person's desires and needs on a personal or social basis. If the pleasing of the other person was his main concern, then he was essentially "taken over" by that person. If he sensed any "toxicity" within that person, any scattered reality as in the Garadene lunatic in Luke 8, then he aggressively blocked that person's influence. If he allowed that person to influence him, then this mission and the mission of Christ through him was thwarted. If he consciously allowed anyone or anything to come in between himself and his Christ, then this was idolatry. For him, there were only two choices: a) the way of the fallen world, or b) the way of the risen Christ. Either way it was an issue of influences and having the discernment to know the difference between them. Charles fought like a Montenegran warrior to stay attuned to the holy and divine influences and remain identified with the mission of his risen Christ. For some of those who were within his sphere of influence, this genuine spiritual warrior attitude was completely foreign, easily labeled within the boundaries of ethnically-biased, social behavior.

While Charles fought tirelessly to remain identified with the *logos* within him, he remained grounded in his humanity. He never lost sight of his humanism, while living in the apocalyptic reality of life on Earth. To Dr. Janzen, a humanist like Charles is one who says to God, "You are God, but I am a human being." Charles always listened for the footsteps of God, while all the time making sure his feet were planted in the earth. Dr. Janzen speaks of Charles' survival in terms of the psyche. He believes that Charles' only true home was in England and Scotland. The British Isles were his psychic home away from home where he sought refuge from the war which only he could see. He could see this war between darkness and light because he had decided to identify himself with the true reality, the *logos* within him. This was a purely internal movement. He chose not to identify himself with a human construction, a manufactured *logos*, therefore freeing himself to realize his potential. Freedom properly utilized.

Yet choosing not to identify with the perishable has its costs. While identifying with the divinizing element within him, Charles remained a human being. During his exile, he remained a son to Radosh and Mileva and a brother to Kossa, Stoya, Dushan and Michael. He continued to be rooted in his humanity while realizing his higher calling to the eternal family of God. This higher calling was a one way street. There was no turning back. The acute pain which he felt from the voluntary separation from his family changed him. This pain, this trial by fire, never really ceased. He never returned to see his parents before they died, nor did he attend their funerals. He never returned to his homeland. [2] He was never to be comforted in his loneliness by his mother or father. The isolation from family was a permanent one, and this affected him. He was never to deviate from his path, never stopping to turn back and concentrate on this separation. The isolation and loneliness changed him. This changed how he saw the world, how he dealt with the world around him. This changed how he related to other human beings.

He did not see others in terms of fitting into a series of social qualifications such as profession, marriage and family. He saw them as fitting into his mission, which he was paying for dearly. His exile changed how he dealt with his wife, his children, his friends, authority figures, his profession, his church, his heart and his God. His exile was essentially a long trial by fire. This fire galvanized the scattered and wayward parts of his inner being, creating the new man, the evolving man. Yet this was a fire which had to be endured, accepted and experienced.

The fire changed him to the extent that not only to his adopted Western world, but also to his homeland and his Orthodox roots, he was of a different breed now, almost unrecognizable. He was an anomaly who did not care that he was an anomaly. He had been burned by the fire, the flame--the primordial flame that lapped at Noah's damp wood as flood waters receded. This fire did not destroy. It purified. Yet there is no process of purification that does not include pain, suffering. This fire, in a sense, lit the way for Charles to find his way to the inner Christ. At that point he was singular in his motivation toward his goal.

This singularity is an oddity in the Western world. It rarely shows itself on the emotional level, where Charles lived and breathed the fine air. This singularity, this accentuated level of concentration, is witnessed on the physical level. Admired and rewarded sports figures are a testament to Western Civilization's continuation of the Roman regard for a well-developed motor skills. The intellectual center is also admired and rewarded, especially in its capabilities to master the postponement of death through modern medicine and the extension of the five senses through science and space exploration, to name a few. Yet the West has rarely seen the likes of someone who has mastered the internal waves. Charles knew that the key to the Gospel teachings of Jesus Christ lay in the mastering of the Legion as described in Luke 8. This mastery is exemplified by the ability to not be affected by the turbulent life of this fallen world. The key is to allow God to act freely through the personality. This means two things: firstly one must realize and maintain this connection with God. Once a task has been realized there is no turning back. It is a lifelong journey. There is no getting rid of God once he has been discovered in the trash heap of the fallen psyche. Secondly, if one is to stay on task, one must not take things personally. When Charles acted out of anger toward an institution, a person or a government, he was not acting on a personal basis. He was acting from within his cosmic task, working diligently to maintain the focus, the order. His cosmic task was to search out those in his midst who sought a higher, spiritual consciousness. This task was wrapped up in a personality that had been battered and bruised by the cruelty and feral nature of the fallen world. For Charles, the conflict between good and evil was a never-ending conflict. World peace was never to be attained as the world existed in its current state. The apocalypse and the new order, the kingdom, this was what he was fighting for.

This trial left him in a constant state of movement. Along with Abraham, he felt like a stranger in a strange land. There was only one place where felt this movement cease, and this place was Britain. England and Scotland were, without a doubt, the adopted home of Charles. He felt indebted to them as a people, as the country who welcomed him when he had no other place to go. In the 1998 journal to his daughter Valerie, he remarked about his love for the British people. He wrote

> . . . I am not an American Citizen, but a British one--chiefly due to my gratitude to [the] British for rescuing me as a refugee in Italy and afterwards educating me for which I am eternally thankful. [3]

In a letter to Professor Arthur S. Herbert following his sabbatical to Woodbrooke College in 1973-74, he writes,

> My year in England was such that I am now passing through the strain of missing my friends there badly as well as the whole ethos of the place, such being the case of my close personal attachment to the country and people. This country is good to me and I am grateful for all the opportunities here. I wish however that Britain was as near as Canada so that I may visit there more often. [4]

On April 1, 1955, Charles signed the certificate to become a naturalized British citizen. It was stamped by the Home Office in Glasgow on April 19 of 1955. The certificate number is BNA 37178.

Notes to "Noli Me Tangere"

1. It is noted among the archives of Charles Ashanin that during his time at Christian Theological Seminary that he directly informed the administration or was planning to produce book-length material on the following subjects:

- Armenian Massacre by the Turks in 1895-96.

- Russian Orthodox Church History

- Church History: vol 1, History of the Early Church vol 2 History of the Patristic Age

- Serbian Saints

His book of essays was published at the time of his retirement in 1990.

2. He had a brief visit with his brother Dushan in Switzerland in 1992.

3. Ashanin, Charles, Valerie's Journal p 42.

4. Ashanin, Charles, Unpublished letter to Prof. Arthur S. Herbert, August 29, 1974.

Alien in an Alien Land

The sense of a perpetual exile continued to permeate every aspect of Charles' life. One of the chief areas that was affected was his relationship with the Orthodox Church, particularly the Orthodox Church in America. It has already been discussed about the "exit interview" Charles had with Bishop Yoanikije as he awaited transport out of Cetije. As Charles remarked in "A Garland for a Mother," this was the last "crutch" from his native land. He did not allow himself to become identified with the organized church, the "outer church," either. Nothing was still. Nothing was stable. In a revealing letter to Norman Cousins at the *Saturday Review* from January 3, 1979, Charles wrote,

One of the reasons which led me to immigrate from Europe to this country was to disassociate myself (because of the deep esteem in which I hold moral and spiritual values of [the] Christian religion), from the corruption of these values due to the privileged position of a State Church which the Communists have justly attacked. Though as you know they have established their own state "Church"! Alas, "The Constantinian privileges" of "Religion" cost the government billions and untold harm is being done to genuine religion and society at large. [1]

Again Charles did not identify with the Orthodox Church, no matter what the form. Yet he remained faithful to the Orthodox faith and its earthly form. He felt strongly called to remain outside the Orthodox priesthood, unlike Georges Florovsky who was a professor and an ordained Orthodox priest. Charles felt very much called to his ministry as a lay theologian. In a letter to Rev. Trevor Wyatt Moore in August of 1971, Charles wrote, "No, I am not in orders, although I hold order in the highest esteem. I am a lay theologian because I feel that must testify to the Orthodox that priesthood is not the only charisma in the Church." [2] Charles had a mission to fulfill. He sought allies along the way. In almost every instance of his life as an exile, he never had a system as an ally. The only system that befriended him was the academic environments at Selly Oaks and Glasgow, his home of body and mind. The other systems consistently and systematically misunderstood or refused to understand the complexity of his existential experiences mixed with a spirituality not based in the intellect.

One glaring issue he had with the Orthodox system was recorded in two April 1972 letters. Since Charles and Natalie took a boat from Africa to Norfolk, Virginia in 1960, they had been members of the Greek Orthodox Church because the Greek church was the only Orthodox Church in Columbia, South Carolina. So when they moved to Indianapolis in 1967, they continued their affiliation with the Greek church, even though they were of Serb and Russian Orthodox backgrounds. During the Paschal Season of 1972, Charles and his family were publicly reprimanded during the service for standing instead of kneeling as the Greek Orthodox were accustomed to do. The day after the incident, Charles wrote a letter to the priest who reprimanded him. He wrote, "I was distressed about your resentment of [a] few people standing instead of kneeling yesterday during the service. As you know these souls do this not to annoy you or to defy your authority, but in respect of the Orthodox tradition which draws our attention to the fact that our Lord is especially close to them during the Paschal season when we sing the triumphant hymn, "Christ is Risen." Please, Father, do respect the Christian conscience of your parishioners even if they seem "crazy" to you. There is so little devotion to our Lord, and those who show it should not be condemned for disobedience." [3]

In a letter three days later to Professor John Meyendorff at St. Vladimir's Seminary, Charles wrote to gain assistance from an ally in the ecumenical spirit he learned in Britain. He tells Dr. Meyendorff of the struggle within the Orthodox Church in America between the inherited and cherished tribal lines drawn long ago. Charles wrote that he had even been asked to leave the Greek Church by a well known Orthodox ecumenist because Charles' "presence challenges the authority of the Ecumenical Patriarchate and the Archdiocese, because of my support of the Autocephalacy." [4] Furthermore, there was the rumor at their local Greek church that Natalie and Charles were there as "Russian spies" since Natalie is of Russian origin.

Charles was vehement in his refusal to join another tribal Orthodox Church (the Romanian Orthodox Church was an option in Indianapolis at the time) because he wanted to be "totally non-ethnic." Charles saw this issue of tribalism within the Orthodox Church in America as an isolating system, bearing the characteristics of Lucifer. [5] In the same spirit as Georges Florovsky, Charles saw the Orthodox Church in America as a regression, a de-evolution, a fearful retreat deeper into ethnic identities. He sensed this when he arrived in Indiana and experienced the beginning of the unraveling of the ecumenical movement at Christian Theological Seminary. In a letter to Dr.

Nicholas Zernov in June of 1968 (one full year after the Ashanin's moved to the Midwest), Charles writes of being distressed over the present state of the Orthodox Church in America. As he began to see it, the same twin spirits of isolation and destruction which were at work at CTS against a sense of true ecumenism, were also at work within the orthodoxy in America. To Charles, by retreating into these ethnic and racial identities, true Orthodoxy was being lost. The more the individual Orthodox groups attempted to salvage, preserve and revive their faith, the more it was sinking into obscurity. Charles wrote to Dr. Zernov about Orthodoxy maintaining itself, so that it can have a unique and distinct message to Christianity and history itself. If it ceases to be itself, then it ceases to be Orthodoxy. Orthodoxy in its legion form of ethnic and racial divisions was nothing short of the demonic masquerading as the divine. This unique masquerading went so far as to claim that it had the spirit of ecumenism. But Charles felt that American Orthodoxy was led by politicians who knew nothing of the ecumenical spirit. He writes to Zernov,

> these are men who are neither disciplined . . . by the family life's discipline nor by ascetic discipline. It is not enough to be a bishop by being a celibate.

> This, as you know, may be a form of highest selfishness. 6

These imposters (what he refers to in his Zernov letter as "Greek chauvinists") speak of ecumenism but, as Berdyaev puts it, it is a "union of disunited." 7

For Charles, true Orthodoxy is true ecumenism, is true Christianity. He writes this hammer blow line to Dr. Zernov; "Ecumenism is only possible by lifting man on the higher level of spiritual consciousness."

Notes to Alien in an Alien Land

1. Ashanin, Charles. Unpublished letter to Mr. Norman Cousins, January 3, 1979.
2. Ashanin, Charles. Unpublished letter to Rev. Trevor Wyatt Moore, August 11, 1971.
3. Ashanin, Charles. Unpublished letter to Rev. Elevterios Lynos, April 17, 1972.
4. Ashanin, Charles. Unpublished letter to Rev. Prof. John Meyendorff, April 20, 1972.

5. In his letter to Prof. Meyendorff, Charles wrote of his dream of starting an "Orthodox *Catholic*, interethnic and interracial mission which we wish to place under the protection of the Orthodox Church in America."

6. Ashanin, Charles. Unpublished letter to Dr. Nicholas Zernov, June 3, 1968.

7. Ashanin, Charles. Unpublished letter to Dr. Nicholas Zernov, June 3, 1968.

What is in a Name?

For Charles it was a constant battle to remain identified with the true *logos*. A true and pure form of temptation comes from this desire, a renamed "need" to become identified with a movement, a cause. This brings a sense of pseudo-belonging. This is termed "pseudo" because it is not based in the eternal, rather it is based in the temporal. The "belonging" to a group, a manufactured cause (and subsequent battle to fight) allows for a sense of direction. Yet if this direction is toward a cause with both feet on earth, then it will leave the member hollow, searching for more. This search, whether it is in a political cause, a family or a religion, is an ancient, human quest. This is the quest toward *permanence*.

As with any true organic symbol, Charles was a human being who lived with one foot on earth and one foot in heaven. Many of his colleagues at CTS considered his private and defensive manner as a sign of guilt over his abandoning his family in Montenegro. Yet his identity was dual, being both with the true *logos* and with humanity. As a human being, he specifically identified himself as a member of the Asanin Clan from the mountains of Montenegro. This dual identity with both the heaven and the earth was trinitarian in nature. He fought hard to maintain his dual nature because he knew that in this was the echo of *permanence.*

It is the opinion of the author that Charles learned much of his ethic of spiritual warfare from his grandfather. In his Journal to Valerie, dated September 7, 1998, Charles wrote an essay entitled "What is in a Name?" He recalled the moment when he was six or seven years old when he chose to inherit and defend the name Asanin. This event is not recorded with any line of detail regarding circumstances and place. One can easily set the scene as being in a plum orchard with a grandfather and grandson walking together and talking in the early afternoon. The grandfather has waited many years for this moment.

Charles recalled his grandfather as having a powerfully gentle presence, yet he also had an equally powerful sense of destiny about him. This early example of presence made a remarkable impact on young Bozidar. He speaks of him as not having given him this sense of heritage. Rather, he speaks of him as offering this heritage to him. His grandfather offered. He accepted.

He taught him much about the aristocratic nature of the Montenegran people who were the descendants of the Serbian Aristocracy who fled after the battle of Kosovo Field in 1389 to the inhospitable terrain of Montenegro. In Montenegro they were able to defend their Christian faith and families from the increasing Turkish and Islamic pressure. As they defended their sense of identity and Serbian Orthodoxy, they developed a code with which they measured their devotion to one another, their heritage and their God. Charles wrote of this code to Valerie, "to achieve this all Montenegrans were bound to each other by a code of *choistvo*--which means a morality based on principle of honor and respect first of oneself and secondly of others who subscribed to this code which is based on the Biblical Ten Commandments of the Old Testament." [1] At this point Charles makes a brief but significant point about the connection between the Montenegran people and the Jewish people. Firstly he speaks of the likelihood that the Jewish people at the time of Moses were a "warrior race." The Ten Commandments "are brief, easily remembered but above all touch all the aspects of communal and individual life which must be observed in order to maintain individual and communal self-respect." [2]

Charles saw this warrior spirit in his grandfather and at age six or seven believed him and resolved to follow this code in his own life. This code was one that was handed down to him through his clan, the Asanin Clan.

The Asanin clan was a member of the family of Montenegro. This fact carried tremendous historical, genetic and therefore cosmic ramifications to Charles and his grandfather. In "A Garland for a Mother" and the essay "What is in a Name?," Charles refers to his grandfather as comparing the Montenegrans to the Levites in the Bibilical Old Testament as both being a people dedicated to the service of the Lord. In "A Garland for a Mother" his grandfather is on his deathbed and confesses his sins to his twenty-four year old grandson. He summarizes his teachings to Charles with a reiteration of the cosmological significance of the Montenegran people. In the text, his grandfather says, "We are a people dedicated to God to be a priesthood of freedom, just as the Levites were given to the service of Jehovah in the Old Testament." [3] In the "What is in a Name?" essay, Charles again speaks of this Levitic connection,

The Ashanin family like all other Montenegran families were a sort of Levitic order--serving the Heavenly Temple in which they lived and offered their sacrifices of the daily toil in a harsh land of stony, inhospitable terrain and cold winters. And although I had to leave that world at age twenty four years old due to the communist assault on the very ethos I have described, I have never forgotten that as one born in Montenegran Serb family, I was bound by the Levitic Service to uphold the Laws of my ancestors wherever I was for my family name of an Ashanin reminded me of that. [4]

This passage from the Journal for Valerie is proof that less than two years before his slumber, Charles was continuing to address the issues of his exile. These issues continued to be identity, loyalty and destiny. In no sense is there any indication that Charles felt that he had betrayed his family or his people. On the contrary, Charles seems to have felt very comfortable with his loyalty to his family name and the Montenegran people. He felt that he was forced to escape the Communist tyranny as well as the tyranny of the state-church within Montenegro. By escaping he did not falter in his loyalty as a Levitic Montenegran. By escaping he preserved his loyalty to this divine calling. In this escape to preserve this line, he maintained this sense that his loyalty to the Levitic Montenegran spirit was indeed a divine calling. One of the hallmarks of the Montenegran-Serb identity in the cosmos is this sense that they are divinely called as a people to be God's defenders of the Holy Light. When tragedy, such as a four hundred year old occupation by a foreign power occurs, this is interpreted (as the exiles of Israel and Judah were interpreted by the Jewish people) as God's divine judgement. These national tragedies are not isolated errors in military strategy and judgement. They are divine corrections. This can only be the case when there is a connection between God and a people in the collective psyche of that people. This connection is the gold that Charles inherited from his grandfather. This inheritance he recognized and chose to accept as his own.

It was one of the sources of energy which propelled him into exile and it was the source of energy which sustained him during his exile. This energy is so rare that it is easily confused with the eccentricities of a human personality. The common paths of our human journey are not accustomed to seeing such focus and attention to maintaining such a connection with a divine destiny. The life of Charles Ashanin gives us a firm indication that destiny does not imply that one no longer has to work toward that destiny because it is already there, awaiting, predestined in some sort. Rather, the life of Charles gives us the indication that destiny is not a foregone conclusion. Destiny, if it is going to be realized, needs to be achieved. This achievement requires attention (nepsis). Destiny can be lost when attention toward the divine *logos* is scattered within one's self. This destiny, which Charles fought to realize is the destiny of all of humanity: recovering our lost connection with the Divine. This is the problem and the tragedy of Adamic man; lost potential and little efforts, unreliability and lack of discernment. Fallen humanity trusts in the tangible, the senses, when the true God can never be seen with eyes that this world gives us. God is experienced only in the wake He makes in the ocean depths. His essence is never experienced, only his energies. His waves we feel, rolling over and around us as we float on the surface of the ocean. Yet God we never see, only the displacement. Like Herman Melville's character named Pip in his epic book on encountering God entitled *Moby Dick*, who experienced seeing God's foot on the great loom as he floated above the depths of the South Pacific.

He surfaced, survived, yet was pulled aboard the Pequod as an insane being, no longer able to experience the world as he once did. [5] Now, the world seemed petty, redundant, inconsequential. The normal reality had been harpooned by the larger reality that this world is indeed not all there is. [6]

There is a larger reality beyond the five senses, beyond what can be experienced in this fallen world of static and confusing background noise. Charles was able to see beyond sight. This ability began when, as a six year old, he chose to accept the cosmic inheritance of his forefathers through the loving guidance of his grandfather. Yet this cosmic inheritance had to be realized on earth, as human beings who work within the framework of history. One of the main reasons Charles was a scholar of early church history lay in this dual nature of humanity with its essence in the cosmic, yet relying on the plane of history to play out this role. History was the wake in the ocean as God passed by, the waves there as proof of God's ultimate reality, the primary essence underneath the surface, foot on the loom, driving creation, calling it home. This was the element that drew Charles to the study of history, because he experienced and understood history as this revelation through his grandfather's guidance and teaching. Through this humanistic apocalypticism, he was in a sense *plugged into the database* of the Serbian and Hebrew people. He was able to "down load" this heritage and translate it into his own modern circumstances. These circumstances included a Balkan Civil War and subsequent Communist takeover and a decision. Charles had to decide how best to preserve and maintain this heritage which he was discovering. The preservation and further cultivation of the Levitic-Montenegran destiny was his goal. In that preservation was his own destiny. To stay in Yugoslavia would have meant certain death. This would mean the end of freedom and freedom is the key element in the realization of one's destiny. Freedom must be preserved.

This was his exile: the preservation of freedom. This was Charles giving the Divine permission to work through him, this being the definition of Divine destiny. Charles chose to be an exile so that he could preserve the freedom which God graced, therefore realizing his own destiny in the universe.

Notes to What is in a Name?

1. Ashanin, Charles. Journal for Valerie, p 47.

2. Ashanin, Charles. Journal for Valerie, p 47.

3. Ashanin, Charles. "A Garland for a Mother" p 92.

4. Ashanin, Charles. Journal for Valerie, p 48.

5. Melville, Herman. *Moby Dick or The White Whale*, The Heritage Press New York, 1943, p 443.

6. Charles Ashanin's last words to the author Dec. 1999; "Those people who think that this world is all there is, those people are so wrong."

The Serb Nationalist

Through his grandfather he inherited this sense that destiny must be preserved in one's life. His grandfather also gave him this sense of preserving destiny regarding the Montenegran people. In the "What is in a Name?" essay, Charles tells Valerie of her great grandfather's participation in the Balkan Wars prior to the First World War. In "A Garland for a Mother," Charles also writes of his grandfather's deathbed confession of two specific instances during his participation in the liberation of Montenegro and Serbia. [1] In these stories, Charles reiterates that his grandfather did not revel in the destruction and chaos of war or the taking of another human life, no matter who or how evil the enemy. The fighting was a necessary part in the preservation of freedom so that family and country could continue the pursuit of their individual and collective destinies. This was the philosophy at the root of Charles' adamant Serb Nationalism. In Coalson Interview 10/29, Charles says plainly that he was a pacifist. He pointed out that he was a pacifist before the war, but after the atrocities he witnessed his pacifism was irrevocable. He recalled a conversation he had with his mother when he was a teenager. "Mother," he said, "I want to defend God." His mother responded, "Son, a God who needs your defense is not worth having him as God. He can take care of himself." This conversation with his mother allowed him to become non-combative with people who are anti-pacifist. He regarded them as childish.

To the Serb, the Serbian people have a collective destiny which began with the Nemanjic Empire. This destiny as a *Christodule* is played out on the stage of history and must be realized, just as an individual's personal destiny must also be played out and realized. Seeking, discovering and realizing a destiny (personally or collectively) was an essential element in the cosmology of Charles Ashanin. His blinding faithfulness to his own destiny baffled those who came in close contact with him. This faithfulness was so strict and narrow that it either repulsed and angered or attracted and calmed. There was no middle ground in your relationship with Charles. Stagnation or direction. Legion or singularity. Death or life.

Purpose in existence was a matter of life and death to Charles. One aspect of his life which was greatly misunderstood was his Serbian Nationalism. At the time of his retirement and subsequent civil lawsuit against CTS, the history of the Balkans ignited again. Charles tells Bob (Interview 1/28) that his retirement coincided with the Yugoslav Civil War. This was so disturbing to him that his scholarly side suffered and he was not able to follow through on his plans to write a book about the 1895-96 Armenian Massacre by the Turks.

The embers of the Second World War had been buried in the ashes by pax-Tito. Tito and his own brand of non-Moscow based Communism had postponed the civil war that had begun in the 1930's. This civil war evolved grotesquely into the Communist takeover. Once the communist regimes in Eastern Europe began to crumble as the Soviet Union spent itself into oblivion, the ghosts of the Second World War were released upon Europe, now fresh and energized after a generation's respite.

This was no more painfully evident than in Yugoslavia in 1991, as the precarious collection of old enemies was finally released from Tito's forced alliance. Slovenia and Croatia soon declared independence, but the populations and borders of Bosnia, Serbia/Montenegro and Croatia were so intermingled and confused, that conflict soon broke out. Between 1991 and 1993 Serbia made great efforts to take control of much of Bosnia and Serbia, all the while fighting against the Croats to the north west. The Serbs were essentially continuing the centuries old struggle against the dual foes of the Catholic Croats and the Muslim

Bosnians. The Muslims were the age-old oppressors of the four hundred year old occupation by the Ottoman Empire. The Catholic Croats were the face of the combative and competitive papal church in Rome. They were also the Nazi collaborators of World War Two called the Ustashis who systematically murdered over 800,000 Serbs in Nazi-esque concentration camps within the borders of Croatia.

This multi-centuried and geographically intertwined history is almost completely foreign to the Americans with whom Charles ministered to and labored beside in Indiana. They were thoroughly unable to comprehend this sense of history which Charles had experienced in his twenties and was still experiencing toward the end of his tenure at CTS and even on into his retirement. For Americans, there is a knowledge of a time before America, but there is no understanding. Protestant Americans have an equally myopic view of the history of Christianity, with the world of Christianity beginning with the rebellion of Martin Luther. It was this myopic view of history which prevented some of his colleagues, acquaintances and friends from understanding his view of the conflict in Yugoslavia. To those not willing to understand Charles as a Serb as well as an Orthodox mystic, he appeared cool, myopic and bitter. Yet to Charles, he cared little about how he appeared to certain people.

All of his exiled years did not diminish his belief in the concept of a Serbian Christodule. This manifested itself in his strong opposition to the U.S. backed NATO intervention in the Bosnian conflict. NATO used a bombing campaign to force Milosovich and the Serbs to the negotiating table. To Charles this was tantamount to the U.S. and NATO supporting the Bosnian Muslims. Charles referred to this bombing campaign as a genocide against the Serbs by the "Christian" nation of the United States.

The Bosnian conflict of the 1990's was not the beginning of his feeling of pro-Islamic stance of the Western powers. In a letter to the Editor of the *Indianapolis Star* on December 17, 1979, Charles writes, "Every historian knows that the spread of Islam and the fire and sword which it unleashed upon the world in the Seventh Century was due to the fact that the Roman and Persian Empires [had] bled each other to death and become both fair play to the Islamic conquest. Islamic followers hope for the repeat, now that they enjoy major economic power in the world." 2

This sense of alarm had flesh put on bone after the collapse of Communism in Yugoslavia. Yet Charles had a firm hope that the West which had so embraced him in his time of need would show equal compassion to the Serbs. In a letter to Professor

William F. Hyland, the Editor of *Foreign Affairs*, Charles wrote of his optimism about the objective compassion of the American people. He wrote, "If my observations of America are right, and I have lived here for only 35 of my fifty years as an exile, the American conscience will revolt against Serbian genocide, for Americans, on reflection, are not bloodthirsty people . . . " [3]

This optimism was a sort of test which Charles gave to people, individually and collectively. You were either for him or you were against him. There was no shade of gray in your relationship with him. This is very evident in the letter to Mr. A.M. Rosenthal of the New York Times after the hopeful letter to Professor Hyland. In the wake of the NATO bombing of the Serbs in Bosnia, Charles writes,

> Indeed, only God alone is able to fathom the depth of iniquity when hundreds of planes from Avianca, Italy, led by American pilots, went to discharge their terror by fire over the Serbs in Bosnia. What did the Serbs do to America that it should treat them so cruelly? . . . My God, Mr. Rosenthal, how far can human duplicity go? Human beings, which your own and my religion considers as God's own creation are treated like ants. What is the difference

> between us and the Nazis? I grieve. I am speechless! Now I know how the Jewish people living in America felt when they heard about their ethnic kinsmen being roasted in Hitler's ovens. [4]

His opposition to the intervention in Bosnia was an issue of justice. The Western Powers and their desires overroad the justice of history of the Christodule of Serbia. Because of the circumstances of history, the Christian West was supporting the Islamic invaders, as he saw it. For him, the implications of this injustice reached far into eternity. In a letter nine months before his death, Charles wrote to the Presiding Jurist of the International Court of Justice in the Hague. He was vehemently objecting to the involvement of the Hague in the prosecution of Serbian war criminals from the Bosnian genocide. He wrote,

Woe to the Earth! On its behalf you have banished justice from the earth. *Deus vedet et judicat!* [God sees and judges] . . . For the Serb people only one thing remains now, to appeal to God and seek divine justice which will judge the unjust "justice' of the world! . . . Woe to the Earth! Your injustice will move Divine Justice to hold responsible those who do not make the justice of the world subject to God's justice. [5]

It is an issue when it is noticed that the injustice which Charles spoke of was also an issue of justice for the Bosnian Muslims as they were experiencing their own genocide at the hands of the Serbs. The Western media was sympathetic toward the plight of the Bosnian Muslims because of the Holocaustian images originating from the Bosnian Serb concentration camps. These images, from camps like Omarska in August of 1992, were vivid reminders that the lessons of history can be overlooked when circumstances prevail over moral duty. [6] These images stirred up memories of a time in the history of Western Civilization that was thought to be isolated, primordial, full of shadows of demons. In a post-holocaust world, the West assumed that media attention was the remedy. As long as the media could spotlight areas of unrest, then genocide could be avoided. To the horror of the West, this was not the case. Concentration camps like Omarska were realities in the former Yugoslavia during the early 1990's. Serbs were also terrorized and murdered by Muslims in Bosnia, yet this was not as dramatically revealed. The Bosnian Serbs were systematic in the form they chose to carry out their genocide. This form, ironically was modeled on the same form the Croatian Ustashi used on the Serbs during the Second World War.

Many of the battle cries used as motivation by the Bosnian Serbs in the 1990's originated in the Serbian genocide of World War Two. Omarska, for example, was a notorious site of a horrific massacre of Serbs in 1941. Omarska of 1992 was revenge for Omarska of 1941. It must be said that many Bosnian Serbs, especially those with an education, fled Bosnia before the ethnic cleansing began. Still other Serbs risked their lives to help Muslim neighbors. Yet the ones who remained and were "caught up" in the orgy of terror were the ones who defined the war and equated the Serbs of the 1990's with the Nazis of the 1930's and 1940's. It was this equating which disturbed Charles. He spent the decade of his retirement being very disillusioned with his adopted homeland. As someone whose life was genetically and biographically rooted in the history of the Balkans, he could not appreciate the lack of a concerted attempt at understanding the history of the Balkans by the Western powers and the Western media. To him this was not an isolated event in Bosnia, nor was the Serbian genocide by the Ustashis. Historically speaking, this conflict was an extension of the one which arose on the Kosovo Plains. Cosmically speaking, this conflict was an extension of the one which began with Nemanja and the dawning of the Christodule in the history of the Serbian people. The conflict was ugly, impure, yet its roots were other-worldly. For Charles, the West had no right to intervene and tip the balance because of the historical circumstances and timing of international attention. The Serbs no matter how gruesome and horrific, were not simply defending geography. They weren't merely recapturing territory for a greater Serbian Homeland. They were defending Serbia, which was defending Christianity from Islam. To the Serb, Serbia is the reason Europe remained Christian in the 14th and 15th Centuries. To the Serb, Serbia is the reason the Christian West was not overtaken and remade into an Islamic civilization. To the Serb, Serbians are warriors. Charles was a Serb.

The cosmology of Charles Ashanin was grounded firmly in a distinct theology of the apocalypse. In an essay he prepared after his retirement entitled, *The Papacy and the Orthodox Church*, he begins with this sentence,

> When I think of the Orthodox Church as a divine outreach in the salvation of mankind, the image that comes to my mind is that of a woman, pursued by the Beast aspiring to kill her and the child she carries within her (Revelation 12). [7]

He goes on to explain how from its inception, the life of the Christian church has been hounded and chased by this beast. The pursuit began after the crucifixion and resurrection of Jesus and subsequent persecution followed in 64 C.E. with the persecution by Nero in Rome, which Charles describes as one of the "most brutal events in the annals of martyrdom in human history." [8]

He then goes into detail about a major aspect of the struggle which he regards as crucial and tragic from the Orthodox viewpoint: the bifurcation of the Church in 1054 C.E. This was the year of "the papal revolution . . . when the Bishop of Rome espoused the imperialist Roman principle and declared himself to be God's Viceroy, first over the Church and then over the world." [9]

Charles extends the case that the Roman Catholic Church has consistently since the split, attempted to weaken and destroy the Orthodox Church as a rival political power. This one thousand year old civil war has manifested itself in the Balkans twice during the twentieth century alone (1940's and 1990's). Charles understood the Roman Catholic Church as growing due to a desire for political power and is therefore too embroiled in the concerns over survival to "be a vehicle of the promised coming of Our Lord to reclaim what is His own from the death and suffering which this world inflicts upon them." [10] Charles writes that this tragic division occurred because the "rebel Church" violated "the ancient principle of *catholicity*." He goes on to write that "Church historians of the early Church testify that the guiding principle of the early Church was not its bureaucracy, but the *General Assembly*, what we Orthodox nowadays call *Sobornost*, a Slavic word which means church members gathering together to deliberate, under the invocation and guidance of the Holy Spirit, matters pertaining to her often precarious precious life, beset as she is by constant attacks of the Devil." [11]

The Orthodox Church has attempted to remain faithful to the practices of the early Church which began on the first Pentecost. At the first Pentecost those present were gathered at a "Sobornost" and received the arrival of the Holy Spirit and the subsequent "anointment." Christ himself puts emphasis on the importance of this gathering in the same Spirit when he speaks of the Advocate being present when two or more are gathered in his Name (Mt. 18:20). It is in this act of gathering which is vital. Firstly, it is an act of humility in that all acknowledge by the act itself that everyone attending is needed in order for the act to exist. The same movement of grace cannot happen by the effort or will of one person alone. Secondly, it is by the repetition of this communal act which is, in a sense, a buildup of energy. This is the energy of grace, the energy needed to fuel the transformation of humanity from a fallen beast to a new creature in Christ (Galatians 6:15). Without this repetition of movements toward God, not enough energy can be gathered. Charles was not interested in dealing with a version of Christianity which did not address the issue of Legion and the fragmented state of the human psyche and subsequently the fragmented state of human civilization. He was not interested in dealing with such cosmic issues on such human terms. He saw the Orthodox Church in Yugoslavia, the Roman Catholic Church and much of Protestant Mainline and Christian Evangelical Right as being cut off from their energy source. The primitive and equally vital issue of basic survival by military, political, social and economic means had risen to the level of an end in and of itself. Economic and political survival in a barbarous, feral world is not the goal of Christianity. Christ's sacrifice was not for the sake of the life of a political institution. There was more to the original source of power which energized the early church. It was this power that Charles was interested in dealing with as an historian of the Early Church and as a human being.

Notes to The Serb Nationalist

1. Ashanin, Charles. "A Garland for a Mother," p 94-97.

2. Ashanin, Charles. Unpublished letter to the Editor of the Indianapolis Star, December 17, 1979.

3. Ashanin, Charles. Unpublished letter to Prof. William F. Hyland, Sept. 12, 1995.

4. Ashanin, Charles. Unpublished letter to A.M. Rosenthal, Sept. 16, 1995.

5. Ashanin, Charles. Unpublished letter to Presiding Jurist of the International Court of Justice, the Hague, Holland, June 3, 1999.

6. Judah. *The Serbs*, p 232.

7. Ashanin, Charles. Unpublished essay *The Papacy and the Orthodox Church* undated, p 1.

8. Ashanin, Charles. *The Papacy and the Orthodox Church*, p 1.

9. Ashanin, Charles. *The Papacy and the Orthodox Church*, p 3.

10. Ashanin, Charles. *The Papacy and the Orthodox Church*, p 6.

11. Ashanin, Charles. *The Papacy and the Orthodox Church*, p 2.

The Cosmic Apocalypticist

In a paper he presented at the Ninth International Patristic and Byzantine Symposium at Princeton University in October of 1989 entitled "The Orthodox Liturgy and the Apocalypse," he begins with these words,

> . . . the Orthodox liturgy discloses the Orthodox spiritual outlook as essentially eschatological. This means that the Orthodox religious mind interprets the world primarily from the eschatological perspective. The reason for this is historical. This has to do with the fact that Christianity was born in essentially a hostile environment. This being the case, Christianity, like Judaism from which it [sprang] was driven to interpret history apocalyptically. By saying this I simply mean that history is a consequence of the cosmic drama which is played out chiefly among the heavenly powers, which do summon human beings to join in

> their fray because they too are a part of this cosmic drama caused by the demonic forces which wage war against their creator. Their rebellion has so effected the earthly realm that it has become subject to their influence and corruption. [1]

In this passage, Charles concisely reasons out his cosmology. He remained loyal to this worldview, as if the image of Lot's wife's last glance constantly played in his mind. Charles remains as a paragon of what it looks like for a human Christian to live eschatologically. He hoped for the future, thereby living fully in the present, hoping for his redemption and the redemption of creation. He consistently fought all "principalities and powers" (Ephesians 6:12) which confronted him. In this sense he was historically and ontologically linked to the earliest followers of the Way. These first Christians of the first three centuries set the tone for the entire religion. It belongs with their history that the true heart of Christianity thrives, like a drumbeat rhythmically echoing into the cosmos. Charles heard this beat and cared little about convincing those who did not hear or did not listen or stopped listening. He trained people how to listen, how to listen to that beat, originating from distant realms, filled with light and life of their own.

Notes to The Cosmic Apocalypticist

1. Ashanin, Charles. "The Orthodox Liturgy and the Apocalypse," published in *The Patristic and Byzantine Review*, vol 9, number 1, 1990, p 31.

The Early Pioneers

In his essay entitled "The Orthodox Liturgy and the Apocalypse," Charles makes specific reference to the social milieu for the early Christians. The imperial cult with its strict Emperor worship did not directly threaten the Christians of the first thirty years following the resurrection of Jesus Christ. The status of Christianity in those days was that of a Jewish Sect, and Judaism was given leniency regarding Emperor worship. This status changed drastically in Rome in July of 64 C.E. This was the beginning of the Neronian persecution. [1]

The groundwork for these persecutions was laid in the suspicious attitude of Roman society toward this mysterious, independent sect since its founder died an inglorious death as a common criminal. According to Walter Oetting in his book entitled *The Church of the Catacombs*, Roman society in general detested the Jews, and the Christians were linked to the Jews. [2] This was a natural conduit of collective hatred. However this general hatred of the Jews seemed to bifurcate and evolve into an intense aberration of the Christians on moral grounds. Oetting writes, "The Christians could show no image of their God and denied the existence of the gods. The Romans deduced from this that they were 'atheists.' When Christians spoke of eating the 'body' and drinking the 'blood' of the 'Son,' the Romans gossiped that they were butchering babies and eating their flesh and blood." [3] In general the Romans viewed the Christians as immoral antinomians. They were dehumanized and easy prey to the blind punches of a dying civilization.

Charles points out that the Jews were also very threatened by Rome and its Imperial cult. The Western conquerors from Julius Caesar through Augustus and his successors fostered the idea of the divinity of the Emperor. Gaius Caligula even attempted to place a statue of himself inside the Temple of Jerusalem. Caligula was assassinated and the new emperor, Emperor Claudius soon restored to the Jews their exemption from the Imperial cult. [4]

Charles goes on to say,

> But Christians were not so lucky. As soon as they were no longer considered by the Romans as a Jewish sect but a separate religion, the weight of the Imperial cult fell upon them demanding their

compliance or total annihilation. This inevitably was understood by Christians as a demonic force seeking to destroy their Messianic claims. [5]

In 64 C.E. there was a tremendous fire in the capital city of Rome. The cause of the fire remains a mystery, yet in its aftermath the Emperor Nero began rebuilding upon the destroyed part of the city. The people witnessed that the new structures were beautiful temples and they accused Nero of causing the initial blaze. To alleviate the political pressure, Nero manipulated the suspicions of the people about the Christians when he blamed them for causing the fire. [6] What followed beginning in 64 C.E. defies description. The writer Tacitus (55?-c. 117) gives these details of the Neronian persecution (Annales, chapter XV, 44),

Besides being put to death they were made to serve as objects of amusement; they were clad in the hides of beasts and torn to death by dogs; others were crucified, others set on fire to serve to illuminate the night when daylight failed. Nero had thrown open his grounds for the display, and putting on a show in the circus, where he mingled with the people in the dress of a charioteer or drove about in his chariot. All this gave rise to a feeling of pity, even towards men whose guilt merited the most exemplary punishment; for it was felt that they were being destroyed not for the public good but to gratify the cruelty of an individual. [7]

Although there is no historical documentation, it is very likely that both Peter and Paul were martyred during the Neronian persecutions.These persecutions, ironically, were not empire-wide until the third century. Nero and the Emperors who followed into the next century simply directed the feral nature of a civilization founded upon the principles of domination and destruction. It was this civilization which demanded a complete and confessed obedience to the emperor. No theology could oppose the Emperor cult. The empire of Rome was based on allegiance and the maintenance of allegiance. It could not exist without allegiance from its members, be they voluntary or involuntary. Christianity was strikingly similar, in that it also demanded complete allegiance of its members to the Man/God Jesus Christ and the body of believers connected through the grace of the Holy Spirit. However, no theology could oppose the Christian God either. To pledge allegiance to the Emperor for a Christian of the first century was the equivalent to eternal suicide. The teachings of Jesus abound in warning of the dangers of beginning on the path and turning away. It was a simple question of heaven or hell. The decision was a conscious one, made in the light of day, while still in the flesh. Stagnation and direction. Legion and singularity. Death and life.

Notes on Early Pioneers

1. Ashanin, Charles. "The Orthodox Liturgy and the Apocalypse," p 32.

2. Oetting, Walter. *The Church of the Catacombs*, Concordia Publishing House, St. Louis, MO 1964, p 88.

3. Oetting, Walter. *The Church of the Catacombs*, p 88-89.

4. Ashanin, Charles. "The Orthodox Liturgy and the Apocalypse," p 33.

5. Ashanin, Charles. "The Orthodox Liturgy and the Apocalypse," p 33.

6. Oetting, Walter. *The Church of the Catacombs*, p 89.

7. Oetting, Walter. *The Church of the Catacombs*, p 117.

The Apocalypse of John

Charles writes that in "this to be or not to be" Christian predicament, the Christian Apocalypse was born. [1] He is referring to the Book of Revelation, which he credits as being a signpost for the early church. John of Patmos was in line with the prophets of the Old Testament such as Isaiah and Ezekiel. John was a seer. This did not mean that he practiced in simply revealing future events. Rather he revealed "the Transcendent Divine Order centered around the throne of Him who abides in his own glory, even God Himself." [2] Upon this throne, the risen Christ sits revealing His victory over sin and death. From this throne goes the Holy Spirit, revealing and binding the body of believers together in one mission: the redemption of humanity and all of creation from the powers and principalities of the evil one. John, speaking specifically to the Seven Churches in Asia, warns them of the dangers of unfaithfulness to the Risen Lord and the task of personal and cosmic redemption. They risk losing their inheritance, won for them by Jesus Christ. Charles links the experience of the persecution in the name of Jesus Christ to the message of the Apocalypse of John;

The Holy Spirit is the source of prophecy and this gift of prophecy is given to Christians, that they may see and know in their persecutions the true reality of God and His Divine order over and against the earthly order which is a false image of the Heavenly order, because the demonic powers which are in rebellion against God have subverted it and established themselves as rulers of the world in opposition to the Creator of the world, the God and Father of Our Lord Jesus Christ. The demonic powers in the guise of the Roman empire, through the person of the Roman emperor, claim God's own prerogative of worship and seek to destroy the followers of the Lamb because they refuse to have the sign of the Beast on their foreheads as do those who worship the Beast instead of God. [3]

While on Patmos, in the middle of the continuing Neronian persecutions, John recaptures the ancient image of the "Lion of Judah," the ever-present Father in Heaven. Through the sacrifice of the Word as Lamb, those subject to the persecution of the Beast are given the freedom from fear and the power to not worship the Beast. They are also given the power through their prayers to cast the Beast into the "bottomless pit." Therefore, the

Apocalypse of John gave the early church, under the enormous pressure arising from the persecutions, the message that not only is God present with them in their struggle against emperor worship, but their suffering is *meaningful.* Through their acceptance of the suffering through the persecutions, they are given the opportunity to participate in the same suffering as their Lord and Savior. They are, in a sense, offered the same door as Jesus Christ. Through this door of suffering, heaven is found. It is the message of Jesus Christ; trust not in the perishable, but in the Light. By trusting in this way of suffering, the early Christians unlocked hidden potential. They chose a direction and did not turn away, even in the midst of horrific suffering. Eusebius writes,

> . . . and on Blandina . . . Blandina was filled with such power that those who by turns kept torturing her in every way from dawn till evening were worn out and exhausted, and themselves confessed defeat from lack of ought else to do to her; they marveled that the breath still remained in her body all mangled and covered with gaping wounds . . . but the blessed woman . . . in confession regained her youth; and for her to say, "I am a Christian,

> and with us no evil finds a place" was refreshment.
>
> 4

Through the acceptance of human suffering at the hands of the Roman Imperial machine, the doors opened for the members of the early church. These doors led to the source of the strength of the Holy Spirit. These early persecutions defined the early church, thus defining the church to come. Charles writes,

> It was fortunate, and in this lies the significance and the grandeur of the Apocalypse that the Christian Church was forced to respond to this challenge and provide a theological and liturgical framework in order to oppose, and not only oppose, but illegitimize theologically Emperor's worship and provide for itself a transcendent and eschatological basis for its own Liturgy, which is based on the Heavenly pattern revealed to the Seer and prophet at Patmos. And it was the Apocalypse which more than any other Christian writing has sustained the Church in its long and bitter struggle of the Church and the Roman Empire up to the time of the Edict of Milan in AD 313 when

Constantine resigned as god to become Vicar of Christ . . . 5

The tone of the Christian religion was set by the second century as a result of the persecutions which Nero began and subsequent Emperor's fostered. This tone is based upon a cosmology that has a fundamental belief that the physical world is a fallen world, subject to the principalities and powers of Satan. In order to rise above and beyond this fallen world, suffering must occur and it must be accepted in the mind of the sufferer. Through this acceptance of the suffering in the name of the Risen Christ, the same narrow path which Christ traveled is taken by the sufferer, therefore opening doors along the way which are otherwise unaccessible. This suffering has a distinct quality to it. The early Christians did not suffer for the sake of suffering alone. They suffered for the sake of Christ, bearing witness to the victory of Christ over death itself (John 11:25-26). To the Christian, this victory cannot be denied. In the fallen world, a mixed world of good and evil, all efforts are made to scatter the mind and foster disbelief in the psyche by the sufferer that the victory Christ has already occurred. As belief is maintained in the mind of the sufferer, the burden is made light, the path made clear and a destiny is revealed. This destiny is reunion with the Creator, as all Christians being wayward particles of the Cosmic Christ are ultimately destined to galvanize into the body of the Redeeming Son of God. This is the meaning of the eschatological nature of Christianity. It is at the very source of the religion itself. Without a proper knowledge and understanding of it, Christianity in its purest sense cannot be attained. Something similar to Christianity can be manufactured to suit the need of a certain group or government. These needs, although well-meaning, only seek to bind and direct on a sociological and political level. They result in transforming it members and their environment into things (Exodus 20:3-6), "its," subjects to be consumed and processed and discarded in the sewer (Mt 7:19). They hold its members within the realm of this fallen world, therefore preventing them from attaining their destined, higher order as that of a child of Light in the image of God (Gen 1:26). Then religion is reduced to a form of social needs and manipulations, therefore preventing it from even functioning as a religion at all. A religion works because it transforms. If a religion does not transform a human being out of the captivity of their animal nature, then it does not function properly and essentially does not exist. Christianity, when truly functioning, must be independent of the dogma of church and state. It is essentially an experiential religion meant to be born within the human heart, with freedom as the catalyst in the fallen world. It cannot be born from without. The experience must be Christ-like, fulfilling every Christian's destiny to have their own personal Golgotha. [6] Suffering and its acceptance implicitly defines the order of the universe for the Christian. It is a decision of monumental proportion with the admission that this world is not all there is, there are realms, unseen and teeming with life. [7] This physical world is only a proving ground, a place of trial, purification. Only in answering to the higher calling of love are we able to pass on to the next level. This answer of "yes" (no matter what the cost) is all that matters.

Yet for Charles, the eschatological aspect of Christian cosmology was not the only primary component. Eschatology was only one side of the coin. Not only was he a cosmic apocalypticist, but he was also a Christian humanist. He beautifully bridged the two aspects in this quote,

> However, God does not abandon the world but seeks to restore it to Himself by exorcising the demonic powers in it. This He does through the Revelation of Himself in Jesus Christ, whereby God Himself acts as His own agent; that is to say, not acting through another but acting directly

> Himself. Christian believers who have and are responding to God's action in Jesus Christ, the Incarnate Word of God are also God's agents in restoring the world to God. As such they are inevitably in opposition to the established order in as much as this order is ignorant of God and His purposes. The earthly order fights against them because it is subject to "principalities and powers, the spirits of wickedness established in high places" and therefore seeks to prevent them from "turning the world upside down." (Acts 4:9) [8]

Charles understood an essential aspect to the belief system of the early church: *redemption*. There are three implicit details to the concept of redemption in the theology of a cosmic apocalypticist. Firstly, there is a hidden, demonic aspect to the life on Earth. The entire milieu of earthly existence is saturated and confused by the principalities and powers of the fallen one, in direct opposition to these redeeming desires of God. To be redeemed means to overcome these powers in the name of the victorious Risen Christ, who overcame death itself.

Secondly, implicit in redemption itself, is the opportunity for a human being to use this opposition by the "established order" of demonic forces. A human being is given the opportunity to use the demonic opposition as a sort of fuel to power them beyond this realm of fallen influences toward the restoration of their psyches and their ultimate salvation. These principalities and powers are not random. To leave them unrecognized is to empower them, to lengthen and broaden their influence.

Thirdly, to be redeemed, to be restored has an essential, implicit, eschatological nature to it. Redemption begs the question 'restored to what form, what condition?' Surely the end of all Christian motives is not simply the return to right behavior. We are called to be restored to a higher life than mere return to a certain action and consequential relationships. We are called to be redeemed, restored, made clean (Mark 7:1-23) from the inside first, then the outward behavior is altered naturally, in its time. This redemption to the higher life means one thing: as Christians we are called upon to overcome death as Christ did and does and will continue to do. Therefore we are called to be deified, living our true eternal life (John 11:25-26) as children of Light, not creatures in the darkness. Archimandrite George Capsanis says, "A God who does not deify man, such a God can have no interest for us, whether He exists or not." [9]

These are the implications of redemption. Redemption is not simply a two-dimensional, theological term. It is a word which contains windows to other worlds. These worlds, demonic and divine lay hidden to those who do not search. But to the Magi of the world, these hidden worlds are revealed and the path to salvation is made clear, its narrowness startling.

Notes to The Apocalypse of John

1. Ashanin, Charles. "The Orthodox Liturgy and the Apocalypse." p 33.
2. Ashanin, Charles. "The Orthodox Liturgy and the Apocalypse." p 33.
3. Ashanin, Charles. "The Orthodox Liturgy and the Apocalypse. p 34.
4. Oetting, Walter. *The Church of the Catacombs*, p 90.
5. Ashanin, Charles. "The Orthodox Liturgy and the Apocalypse." p 35.
6. Quote from a 3-27-98 conversation between author and Charles Ashanin.

7. Quote from a December 1999 conversation between author and Charles Ashanin.

8. Ashanin, Charles. "The Orthodox Liturgy and the Apocalypse." p 31-32.

9. Capsanis, George. *The Eros of Repentance*, Praxis Institute Press, Newbury MA, p 15.

The Christian Humanist

During the season of Pentecost in 1988, Charles and Natalie undertook a pilgrimage to the Soviet Union to celebrate one thousand years of Orthodoxy in Russia. This was a monumental journey on several levels. It was important for Charles to honor the influence of Natalie's family within his own life. In an essay published in the journal *Logos*, Charles writes, " . . . perhaps the greatest debt I felt to the Church, was for nurturing in the Orthodox faith the family of my wife, Natalie, whose tradition of spirituality and love for Christ she brought to our marriage. Her granduncle, Archpriest Peter Otdelnoff, was martyred by the Bolsheviks." [1] This was an important trip as a fellow Orthodox, giving thanks and gratitude to the Russian people for being the key ally of the Serbian Orthodox as they endured the four hundred year Turkish occupation. This gratitude was culminated in the privilege to take Holy Communion in Communist Russia. This was also a key event in his life due to the physical journey itself. On August 24th of 1984, Charles underwent double by-pass heart surgery. It had been discovered that twice in the 1970's he had had a heart attack. These had been misdiagnosed as a hiatal hernia. 2

In his sixty-eighth year, a trip of such distance was no small affair. This trip also had tremendous significance for him as he traveled voluntarily into THE Communist State. His entire exile was fueled by his escape from the Communists in Yugoslavia. He had not returned to Yugoslavia for fear of his own capture and most probable imprisonment or execution. Indeed, the reason he changed his name to Charles was to hide his identity from Tito's agents. To travel to the Soviet Union was a physical and psychological risk. He writes about his Russian pilgrimage,

But the problem for me was, how could I possibly bear to reenter the communist world and visit a country which has spawned the communist pestilence in the world; one which has brought so much anguish to so many. Because communism, I was not able to attend the funerals of my parents, much less to visit them for 40 years. Exile and those who inflict it on others leave deep scars on their victims. [3]

Soon after returning from his pilgrimage he sat down for a television interview with his dear friend Ted Nottingham. This interview is entitled, *Turning Toward the Light.* Charles tells the story of meeting a Russian journalist at a reception at Northwood

Christian Church for Russian Christians involved in the Peace March. The journalist asked Charles, "what kind of God is their God?" (meaning the American Christians) Charles replied, "Well, our God is a good God. He is an ethical God, who demands that certain norms be observed. I think you know already what those are. It is wonderful to know that we worship a good God, who is known for His goodness. So we strive to be good, because we worship a good God," I said. "We may not be individually good. But all of us want to be good." 4

He goes on to say that the God of the Orthodox is also a "good" God, yet this is not God's chief characteristic to which humans relate. For Charles, God's chief characteristic is that of holiness. The way in which we relate is adoration. Russian churches for instance reveal this adoration in their gold domes even though they are a poor country. Charles goes on to say,

> What is adoration? Adoration is leaving yourself to the glorious result without any conditions. Americans are a rationalistic people who are not prepared to go that far. American Christians say to God, "We want to have covenant with You. We want to honor You. We want to do Your will.' As

> Bishop Anthony Bloom said, "I always pray, 'God, ask anything of me–but not the Cross.'" [5]

Then Charles makes the following statement, "You cannot have a relationship with anyone without imposing upon your own life a demand of self-sacrifice." [6] True union with God expresses itself most eloquently in the Crucifixion. For Charles the Crucifixion is not an imposed event by a distant God, rather "it is a revelation of the sacrificial love of God on our behalf and our response to him in the same kind of attitude." [7]

Charles continues in the interview,

> I learned this by reading the works of Maximus the Confessor and other ancient Christian mystics. They say that we human beings are the union of physical matter and the divine Spirit. Thus, we are priests to the universe. We are intercessors between the universe and God. By virtue of our physical nature and by virtue of the fact that God's Spirit lives within us, we are able to bring nature to God and able to bring God to nature. In an unrestricted sense, then, we enter into the process of Creation and into the life of the Divine. [8]

Ted Nottingham poses the question, "That unrestricted entrance is what the Orthodox call theosis, or divinization?" Charles responds, "Theosis refers to this process, this "Christique" whereby we are called into becoming the sons and daughters of God through Jesus Christ. I might add a personal note: four years ago, I had open-heart surgery and found myself on the boundary between life and death. Yet, being on that boundary, I was aware of a dimension of being that I earnestly sought. I wanted to punch through the boundary, but something was pulling me back to earthly existence. I interpreted this to be the prayers of my friends, drawing me back. That experience of being "on the boundary" makes me aware of a transcendent ocean of love, of goodness, of truth, that is behind us in our pilgrimage, assisting us to embody within our earthly life enough of that vision to transform this existence into its likeness." [9]

What follows next in the interview is the heart of the theology of Charles Bozidar Ashanin. This passage is proof of his Christian Humanism;

> This is my hope for the world: let us use our talents to celebrate and testify to that vision. The artist should paint images, the poet should compose

> poetry, the musician should make music to celebrate this vision. Each of us individually in our earthly life should share with each other sacramentally something of that vision, to enable each other's life by the gift which He has given to each one of us. We cannot receive that gift and keep it to ourselves. We must share it with each other. This is the Eucharist of the self-sacrificial love of God on behalf of Creation, and especially of us human beings, whom He loves. [10]

For Charles, Christianity was unique to the universe because of its "Christique" character. Within this character, the personality of Christ speaks to each individual personality within a human being. The Christ in Jesus beckons the Christ in each human being. This beckoning is toward true life. We are each called to become a fully realized, particle of the Cosmic Christ, realizing our destiny: to become divinized. We are not meant to become carbon copies of Jesus of Nazareth. Rather, we are called to be a fully realized version of Christ, pertinent to that moment in the development of Creation. What this means is that to be a Christian means to work in this lifetime to develop fully our own personality, which Charles points out used to be termed the "soul" or "human spirit."

Charles says, "this concept of human personality exerts itself as a task and a responsibility, rather than as something finished once and for all. We are not made perfect, but we are made such that we can realize perfection." [11] For Charles, the human personality is a gift to be realized during a life time of effort. All of life is the education. Life, true life is a process of becoming. This brings into perspective the issue of purpose and direction; to know and understand that true life has meaning only when it is focused toward God. This focus toward God is not only a linear focus in terms of an eschatological issue, but is also linear in its development of each individual, human personality. This dual focus gives meaning to life itself. This meaning is only realized when a person becomes aware of the Christ within them, and then aware of the Christ everywhere in the cosmos. This awareness brings with it a great responsibility and an even greater danger if it is discovered and then subsequently ignored (Luke 9:62). Charles was able to balance a theology of Cosmic Apocalypticism with an equally vibrant theology of Christian Humanism. He was a living symbol, existing with one foot in the heavens and one foot on earth.

It is best now to finish with an examination of his theology of Christian Humanism. It is here that he is grounded firmly, taking his place in the ranks of the Cappadocian Fathers of the Third and Fourth Century Byzantium.

Notes to The Christian Humanist

1. Ashanin, Charles. *Essays on Orthodox Christianity and Church History*, p 215-216.

2. Ashanin, Charles. *Valerie's Journal.* p 26.

3. Ashanin, Charles. *Essays on Orthodox Christianity and Church History*, p 225.

4. Ashanin, Charles. "Turning Toward the Light," video interview with Ted Nottingham, Disciples of Christ, 1988 transcript page 7.

5. Ashanin, Charles. "Turning Toward the Light," p 7.

6. Ashanin, Charles. "Turning Toward the Light," p 8.

7. Ashanin, Charles. "Turning Toward the Light," p 9.

8. Ashanin, Charles. "Turning Toward the Light," p 9.

9. Ashanin, Charles. "Turning Toward the Light," p 10.

10.Ashanin, Charles."Turning Toward the Light," p 10.

11.Ashanin, Charles."Turning Toward the Light," p 11.

A Cappadocian Father

God became man in order that man may become divine again.

-- St. Anthanasius

One of the unique qualities of Charles Ashanin was his ability to have dual attention. By this we mean his attention on the Divine within himself was intense enough to address the Divine within his world. This meant that when he spoke with you, he was not only speaking to your personality, but the Christ within himself was communicating beyond comprehension with the Christ within you. This resulted in a very intense sense of concentration. If one's personality was open to this level of communication, then the encounter was beyond the normal chatter of our surface existence. This encounter had the potential to touch one in a deep manner, causing a remembrance of a long forgotten part of one's being. This part of one's being was suddenly awakened, communicating its divine nature to the long-slumbering psyche. He tells Bob in an interview two weeks before his death that he thought of himself as a quarryman whose job it was to seek out potential stones for the artist to sculpt. These speaking stones were his allies in this cosmic battle. These allies were the ones who made the necessary efforts to listen to their inward Christ. This mission rose above the realities of human relatedness. His exile caused him to be amazingly dedicated to defining the family in terms of the inward, spiritual connection. His definition of family was not confined to an immediate, genetic family.

It must be reiterated how amazing his ability was to see beyond the realities of familial, social, ethnic and religious definitions. Here was an Orthodox Montenegran born in 1920 who at the age of twenty-four was able to see beyond the cataclysmic nature of the combined realities of a simultaneous civil war which was systematically isolating and destroying his entire family and country as he knew it. He escaped intact, yet scarred. Beyond the realities of the nature of his inward scars, we see a beauty that emerged because of the trauma. Not unlike a birth, Charles survived, now being exposed to the new life. This new life had its dangers, but he had gone too far to turn back. He knew too much of this new life and its possibilities.

Charles was the pre-imminent teacher. This was the human, social form of his mission on Earth. He was a University of Glasgow trained Early Church Historian with the heart of a theologian. The term theologian is used here as Gregory of Nazianzus defined it, not as one who excels in scholastic discourse, but as one who prays. [1] Charles prayed people toward God. The professional and social form of his activity was teaching. Charles had a unique, non-linear, essentially non-Western style of teaching. He would lecture to his students with no notes, eyes closed and often times arms raised.

Charles had a method of education behind his teaching style. Behind his method and his personal style was a philosophy of Christianity shaped by his personal trial by fire in his exile and the divine reality that had been awakened within him. This philosophy was a combination of Cosmic Apocalypticism and Christian Humanism.

Charles was keenly interested in the concept and application of Christian Humanism in relationship to the study of the history, theology and culture of Western Civilization. He was interested in the evolution of Western Culture in the context of a distinctive and vital synthesis between classical Greek antiquity and early Christianity. In short, he was concerned with the possibilities of humanity's evolution. For Charles, the next evolutionary step for humanity was not the realm of the body, but that of the psyche, or the soul's movement toward becoming a Spirit. He saw a perfect synthesis of the method of Greek Paideia (the Greek method of education) and the content of Christianity. He saw this method and content existing within the context of Western Civilization itself. This combination was for him the proper answer to the question of man's ultimate purpose on earth. Without the practical method for the learning of the content, then humanity flounders within a culture, remaining a beast, an animal only concerned with its own immediate needs and misguided desires. The combination of the method of education within the Greek Paideia and the content of the message of Jesus Christ gives a potent answer to the problem of humanity's purpose, namely to realize their true form (Genesis 1:26). Charles knew the practical realities of this process of deification. He knew that it is achieved on a personal basis yet must be supported by a method that is endorsed and defended by a society and its culture.

Charles believed that the foundation of Western Civilization itself was based in *humanism*. One of the most significant works of scholarship which Charles produced was an essay entitled "Christian Humanism of the Cappadocian Fathers," which was published in 1987 in the Patristic and Byzantine Review. In it he expounds upon his understanding and appreciation of the original concept of humanism and the role that it played in combining the philosophies of classical Greek antiquity with early Christian theology through the fifth century. Early in the essay, he points out what humanism is by stating what it is not. He says that humanism in its modern context has lost its meaning. He writes,

> In our own time, especially in America, the idea of humanism is riddled by ambiguity so that in the Christian circles it has become often devalued and misunderstood to the point that it is forgotten that there is no genuine Christianity without Humanism nor genuine Humanism without Christianity. This crisis is evident in the conflict between the so-called religious and secular elements in our culture which is manifested in the science vs. religion controversy, or that of Christianity vs. Secular Humanism! But Secular Humanism is a misnomer, the proper name for it is *Hominism* so aptly named by Geddes Mcgreggor in his book: *The Hemlock and the Cross: Humanism, Socrates and Christ.* The adherents of this school are referred to as Hominists whom he describes in delineating them

> from Humanists in the classical sense as those who "have no distinctive faith in the potentialities of the human race. They have no belief in a human nature that possesses certain intrinsic and inalienable characteristics or qualities. In short, they have no doctrine of an essential nature of man." [2]

He goes on to write, "hominism . . . . reduces everything to the realm of nature and thus condemns human beings to mere psychology, sociology, and biology, while humanism releases them into the world of personality where the spirit unleashes the imagination which the *logos* forms into ideas by means of which human beings contemplate God as the source of freedom and creativity." [3]

In this essay, Charles draws heavily from the scholarship of Werner Jaeger for an understanding of the vital synthesis between the Greek Paideia and Christianity. Charles writes, "In his great work *Paideia: The Ideals of Greek Culture*, perhaps the finest work written on this subject during our century, Werner Jaeger writes: 'The intellectual principle of the Greeks is not individualism, but "humanism," to use the word in its original and classical sense. It comes from *humanitas*. It meant the process of educating man into his true form, that is the real and genuine human nature.

This is the true Greek Paideia, adopted by the Roman statesman as a model. It starts from the ideal, not from the individual.'" 4

This concept of the ideal within the individual explains the model by which Charles worked. He appreciated Jaeger's view that the Classical Greek's greatest work of art was Man himself. 5 Knowledge of and about one's innermost heart is the prime objective of those who have ears to listen. It unfolds in one's life like a map slowly revealed, yet uninterpreted. Self-knowledge is indeed the vocation of all vocations. It lives and breaths as a voluntary objective, beckoning and tempting in one simultaneous motion. It beckons us, reminding us that our true nature remains unrealized and we are essentially a cartoon of a true human being. It tempts us, speaking to the loose collection of fragmented, desperate selves within one human life.

This process of self-realization was the driving force behind the philosophy of education of Charles Ashanin. For him, those who had ears to hear were those who were embarking or had embarked upon the journey of realizing one's true nature. These human beings were his allies in the fight toward the true Light. Charles was to be forever interested in this process, what he would term "the reeducation of mankind." This reeducation of mankind needed a method. This method was the Greek Paideia.

It was the embodiment of the Greek philosophy of humanism. The classical Greeks believed that humanity, in its present, undeveloped condition needed a method in order for the development to take place. The Early Church Fathers of the second and third centuries knew that within the teachings of Jesus Christ was held the secrets of obtaining self-hood or true human nature (humanism). Yet they needed a method of realizing this nature, essentially a method of psychological evolution was sought and found in the principles and methods of the Greek Paideia. Charles cites Dr. Jaeger's work *Early Christianity and the Greek Paideia* as tracing the process of synthesizing the Greek Paideia and Christianity as early as the New Testament in "the Epistles to the Ephesians, Hebrews and II Timothy, but especially in the First Epistle of Clement of Rome to the Corinthians. For him [Jaeger] Clement's Epistle is proof how much the early church concisely or otherwise was imbued by the ideals of the Greek Paideia." [6]

Some other sources of evidence that the early church adopted the method of the Greek Paideia are the *Epistle of Diognitus* and *Octavius of Muncius Felix*, Tertullian's *Apologeticum* and Clement of Alexandria. Charles understood that Clement especially was one who "saw clearly that the recognition of the Greek Paideia was essential to Christianity as a vehicle for its mission of the reeducation of mankind in the Spirit of the Gospel. The conflict of Christianity with paganism notwithstanding, it was clear to Clement that Greek Paideia should be rescued so far as Christianity was concerned from the religious paganism of the time. Greek Paideia in his mind was the finest educational method and Christianity needed it and he boldly claimed it for Christianity." [7]

The Greek Paideia was essentially remade into a new form, making it a Christian form, thus giving it freedom from any further instruction from the Greek source. Likewise the early Church fathers essentially remade the Septuigant into a new form, making it a Christian form, thus also giving it freedom from any further instruction from the Jewish source. At this point the Christianity of the second and third centuries stated its independence from the key influences of Judaism and Classical Greek culture. The early church had boldness and wisdom in it willingness to draw out the truest content and finest method from other cultures and religions.

This process of acquiring a method for the most effective application of its content began soon after the ministry of the Apostles and Paul ended. As has been stated already this process was taken up by the likes of Clement of Rome, Tertullian and

Clement of Alexandria. The full maturation of this process was seen through by the Cappadocian Fathers in the East in the fourth and fifth centuries and later by Augustine in the West. It was during the fourth century that this process of maturation took place from the Greek Paideia to the Christian Paideia. The classical humanism of the Greeks was essentially altered by the new content and transformed into Christian Humanism, yet the method remained the same. Charles points out two systematic achievements that the Cappadocian Fathers made. Firstly, beginning with St. Basil who was following in the footsteps of Clement and Origen, the case was made that Christian education should not be confined to just Christian writings. The ethic being used was teleological in that the prime objective of Christian education was the promotion of the development of personality. Whatever author promoted the development of true character was therefore suitable for study. The key was the goal itself which was the evolution of a human being from a needs-driven animal to a life-serving god. Secondly and most impressively was the fact that the Cappadocian Fathers of Basil, Gregory of Nazianzus and Gregory of Nyssa pulled off an "intellectual coup," by taking the Rhetoric expression of the classical Greek Paideia and making it into a Christian form of Rhetoric. The Cappadocian Fathers took the argument by Libanius and other Pagan Rhetoricians that Christianity was an anti-humanistic religion and argued that

Christianity was actually the only humanistic religion. Without it, Rhetoric speaks to the vanity of the human situation without any concentration on the promotion of the personality. Charles writes,

> By this intellectual Coup, the Cappadocians, all of them Rhetoricans *par excellence* both by education and by native genius, have committed themselves and Christianity not only to the Humanism of the Greek Paideia, but have given to this humanism higher consciousness as the search for a new vision of human destiny as revealed in Christianity, where human personality stands as a new revelation of the humanist vision, not just as an ideal humanity, as in the classical humanism, but as an ideal which finds its embodiment in the Person of Jesus Christ, through Whom and in Whom human quest and the humanist tradition of the past finds its embodiment its goal as well as the inspiration for the pursuance of it s quest towards better future for humanity. [8]

The Cappadocian Fathers were not interested in some of the aspects of Greek Paideia such as grammar and logic, rather, they were interested in its imagination, "its Sophia." [9] The heretical movements such as the Arian, Semi-Arian, Homean, Anomean, Appolinarian, Eunomian and Macedonian were all essentially *hominist*, as far as Charles was concerned. They did not give full expression, which to Charles equalled full justice to the doctrine of humanity. The heretics were heretical in that they did not fully express the "Christian Humanism of the Christian Revelation." [10] The early church was able to discern that it needed the gnoseology of the Greek Paideia but not its tools of epistemology. [11] It saw a distinction between epistemology and gnoseology which was of interest to Charles, as evidenced by an unpublished and undated essay entitled *The Nature of Theological Thinking (A Problem Of Epistemology and Gnoseology).* In this essay he briefly discusses how epistemology and gnoseology are at the same time unified and yet distinctive from one another.

The goal of the theologian and the philosopher is that of the "knowability of being." [12] Knowability is more than using the five senses to register whether an object or an experience has been experienced in a similar fashion. Charles is not interested in the blatant registering of the reality of objects by empirical observation. He is interested in the issue of the ramifications of an encounter with another person. He believed that when two persons have an encounter a simultaneous action takes place.

Epistemologically, these two persons encounter one another in terms of the interaction between their physical nature, i.e. they experience one another through their five senses. Charles regards this as a passive experience, not demanding anything from the participants for its comprehension. Gnoseologically and more importantly, the two encounter one another in terms of a dynamic reality. This dynamic reality rises above the mere comprehension through the five senses. This dynamism controls the situation by its ability to create. Suddenly a human being is not acting, he or she is being acted upon. The interaction is not predictable through empirical observation. It leaves man with a choice to reject it or accept it. Upon accepting it, a higher reality unveils itself, a transcendent reality. Charles writes,

> Trust, faith in, point to the fact that reality is not here to be snatched at but rather lived as an encounter of I and Thou, as a necessity of human existence inasmuch as it wants to be a subject and not an object, a person not a thing. Here it becomes evident that our knowing of objects and persons demands also different terms in describing these two ways in which being becomes known to man. Thus the theologian is justified when he assigns to epistemology the right to discuss the

> possibility of objective knowledge, i.e. the knowledge of things, and to gnoseology knowledge of personal reality. [13]

The Early Church Fathers, especially the Cappadocian Fathers understood that what they were undertaking was "the metamorphosis of Classical Humanism into Christian Humanism." [14] What they needed this for was not the Greek method of knowing things and objects. Rather, they wanted to use their method of understanding the personal encounter. They understood that each individual is starkly responsible for their own salvation, having understood and responded to the act of God's grace through Jesus Christ. Each personality contains within it the unique expression of God's presence. The key is the *re-education* of the individual in order to best express this Holy Element within them, thus realizing the very act of evolution itself; the inward evolution which Christ revealed to the world. The goal of this re-education or evolution is theosis or deification, which is the missing piece to the broken puzzle of modern Christianity. The Christian Paideia is vitally important to the progress of Christianity into a world religion because it allowed Christianity to speak to the hope within humanity. This hope is that within us all there is memory, a holy reminder of the particle of Christ within us. In order for this to be rediscovered and developed fully, making it a prepared and functioning particle ready for the larger body of the Cosmic Christ, we must individually and collectively participate.

Individually speaking we must allow our personalities to be developed fully; i.e. humanism and Paideia. The talents and characteristics must be discovered and used to their fully capacity. This is the influence of the Classical Paideia which we still see in our general philosophy of education in the West as expressed through our high schools and universities where a general core of subjects is required of all students. This is why Charles was an educator. He loved to see personalities develop fully. He loved to see his students awaken to this personal awareness of the "bliss within them", as Joseph Campbell so eloquently said. There is an element of sheer joy and happiness when someone discovers that their purpose in life coincides with what they enjoy, their talents, their love. They discover this bliss, this guiding purpose, this element which galvanizes their inward purpose with their outward, human expression of it with the created world of civilization. Charles loved to see a student "fit it" to their world, participate and contribute. For him, the teacher, he knew that the human life is not truly human until it functions fully as God intended. Our true nature needs to be realized. We need to be a healthy, fully realized particle of Christ, therefore the Christian Paideia assists the process of theosis by recognizing that the development of the personality is a key issue in the entire process. The Early Church Fathers recognized that there is not theosis, no salvation without the development of the personality, hence the acceptance of any author who promotes the edification of character. This is where Charles found his bliss, in the role of the teacher who opened new worlds to his students. This world was essentially a path, a journey back to God. This journey begins in the flesh, but ends in the Light.

Charles understood that the appreciation of the importance of gnoseology was the key to advancing toward theosis. The reason gnoseology was so vital, hence the Paideia itself, was because this journey back to God does indeed begin in the flesh. By this we mean that what happens to us as human beings is a key element to our whole evolution. More importantly, our true evolution occurs in proportion to how well we process what happens to us as human beings. The life that we live, whether it be passive activities or assertive actions in the world of people and objects, affects how we perceive or don't perceive this particle of Christ within us. These issues all find action within the fallen world where good and evil inter-mix. In order to see clearly this holy element within ourselves we need to experience, as it were, a series of births, so that we may pass on to the next stage of development, the humanism of the Christian Paideia all the while undergirding this process with purpose and direction. Charles felt that who he was in the flesh was not who he wanted to be.

Notes to The Cappadocian Father

1. Ashanin, Charles. "Christian Humanism of the Cappadocian Fathers," published in *The Patristic and Byzantine Review* vol 6 number 1 1987, p 52.

2. Ibid p 46.

3. Ibid p 47.

4. Ibid p 45.

5. Ibid p 46.

6. Ibid p 48.

7. Ibid p 48.

8. Ibid p 49.

9. Ibid p 51.

10.Ibid p 51.

11.Ibid p 52.

12.Ashanin, Charles, "The Nature of Theological Thinking (a Problem of Epistemology and Gnoseology) unpublished and undated, p 1.

13.Ibid p 2-3.

14.Ashanin, Charles. "Christian Humanism of the Cappadocian Fathers" p 52.

Three Births

Introduction

In an undated essay initially delivered as a lecture given at CTS, Charles discusses the issues involved in the process of realizing true personhood and the divinity within one's being. The essay is entitled *The Problem of the Three Births of Man*. Within this essay itself, Charles finds a magnificent rhythm, and soars as both a humanist and an apocalypticist. This is one of his finest moments as a scholar and a sage. We will discuss its importance to his life and theology beginning with the essay's opening three paragraph's which give us the tone of Charles' spirit.

Gregory of Nazianzus was a Church Father of the Fourth Century. In addition to being a great theologian and highly educated man of his age, he was also a spiritual leader of the Catholic Church of his time and a great poet. In one of his poems, entitled "To Vitalian from His Son," he writes:

'By his first birth of flesh and blood man arrives on earth and quickly disappears; Then comes the second birth of the Holy Spirit when the Light (from on high) descends upon him as he is washed by the water of baptism. The third birth through tears and sufferings makes clean (God's) image in us which has been obscured by evil. The first of these births we have from our fathers, the second from God and the third we ourselves are the authors, appearing to the world like a grateful light.' (P.G. XXXVII, 1948 a-1999 a) I was struck by these thoughts and I would like to discuss them with you under the title, "The Problem of the Three Births of Man," for I believe that all the psychological drama of man to which you as agents of pastoral care are called to minister, centers around these three problems; man's relationship to his parents, i.e. the problem of his physical birth; man's relationship to God, the problem of his spiritual birth; and man's relationship to himself, the problem of *his selfhood's birth*, so deeply bound up with man's relationship to himself. [1]

Initially, he gives as a definition of birth for his purposes as "becoming an independent entity." This entity which he speaks of is the personality itself, because this is what differentiates human beings from one another. Charles says explicitly, "Personhood and personality we must say is a never fully realized fact in man's earthly existence but it is something towards the realization of which he is driven by evolutionary trust of his inner being. Personality or personhood is realized by man only in a degree, never in an absolute sense." 2 This is where Charles distinguishes himself as a Christian Humanist; being a Christian means being fully human and fully divine, as shown in the life and resurrection of Jesus Christ. This process is called theosis or divinization by the Early Church Fathers. This process begins with a human being struggling within a lifetime toward a true independence from his or her parents, God and lastly himself or herself. Let us first discuss the issue of being born from one's parents.

Notes to Three Births; Introduction

1. Ashanin, Charles. *The Problem of the Three Births of Man* unpublished p 1.

2. Ashanin, Charles. *The Problem of the Three Births of Man* p 1-2.

Birth One

In his essay on the three births of man, Charles pays homage to the influence which Christianity played in moving the pagan world out of its viewpoint that children were personal property. Yet he also acknowledges the fact that the issue of freedom from one's parents is an amazingly far-reaching and subtle problem for society as a whole. Charles addresses this problem again in terms of epistemology and gnoseology. He writes, "Before a person could be born from his parents, emancipated from them, he must be reconciled with them. What do I mean by this? It is not helpful to a person to just cut himself forcibly away from his home, running away both in the physical and psychological sense does not help. To liberate one's self from one's parents, to be born from them, it is necessary to "objectivize" one's parents, to see them psychologically outside of one's own life, related to them by the bond of all that parents are and mean to us, but as beings who can and must, in the final analysis, exist without us and we without them." [1]

For Charles, the key is to admire one's parents, but disengage in worship of one's parents. The admiration means being able to see "the value of something in its own right." This means further that one recognizes characteristics of the personality of the parent as characteristics that they themselves want to emulate. But it is in the recognition of these characteristics by the child which makes all the difference. They must rise from within the child, not be forcibly tacked on to the outside. One of the hallmarks of humanist philosophy is the guidance arising from within a human being, a recognition, a remembrance of union of personality and spirit.

Charles writes that, "the best way to be born from one's parents in the sense of being liberated from their psychological tutelage and dominance is to see them and ourselves as related primarily, not to each other, but to God through whom we are interdependent upon each other." 2 This is how Charles was able to leave his parents at age twenty-four and never return. This is how he was able to leave them behind and yet remain connected to them. This connection (rising above and beyond the epistemological to the gnoseological) was of primary importance because it was an act of liberation, not a two-dimensional, philosophical idea. He was connected to his parents via the Spirit of the Triune God, not just the genetic relationship between child and parents. This cosmological relationship liberated him from the bondage of sentimental duties. In other words, he would not allow the expectations of familial obligations and ethnic and religious responsibilities to override his own sense of relationship to God. For it was this relationship to God which was his ultimate concern, the ultimate goal being reunion with God. Even though Charles was a staunch Serbian Nationalist when it came to political expression, ultimately this was all founded in the collective mission as a Christodule or a servant of Christ on Earth. He never supported Serbian Nationalism as an end in and of itself. Serbian Nationalism was a means to a greater cosmic end. He saw both personal and global issues in the widest context possible, that of spiritual reunion with the creator God.

This was especially difficult for his colleagues at CTS to comprehend after the spirit of ecumenism began to abate and Liberation theology began to take root. Christianity was being reduced to the imitation of right behavior. For Charles, right behavior had to arise from within, as it were, a remembered act instead of an imitated one. This meant that the heart must be prepared and all pretenses, all illusions must be forcibly rooted out. The one, universal battle that we must all deal with is that of the liberation from our parents. Charles knew this and was successful in his birth from his parents.

Notes to Birth One

1. Ashanin, Charles. *The Problem of the Three Births of Man* p 2.

2. Ashanin, Charles. *The Problem of the Three Births of Man* p 3.

Birth Two

One of the keys to understanding Charles' inspiration for his lifelong exile was his identification of and understanding of the neo-paganism of Nazi-Fascism and the atheism of Communism. Primarily within the atheism of Communism he envisioned a horrific future. Even if he physically survived the ultimate takeover by Tito's version of Soviet Communism (which he witnessed as a greater threat than Hitler's Fascism), Charles saw, in a sense, a spiritual and physical death mark placed upon him. He saw atheism as a major threat to the foundation of all that Christianity proposes; i.e. the full realization of one's humanity and divinity.

Following the first birth as being the objectivization of one's parents, Charles goes on to describe the second birth as being the birth of man from God. This second birth is why he opposed the theology of atheism so vehemently with a lifelong exile. For Charles the understanding of atheism begins with the presupposition of God's nonexistence. One of his most important sources for an understanding of atheism and therefore humanism was again in the prophetic writings of Fyodor Dostoevsky. He specifically refers to Kirilov in *Crime and Punishment*, who experiences life as rules by logic and reason, a world in which God does not exist. If God does not exist, then man must be God. If man is God then man exists on Earth as the dominant force over life itself, choosing by his own volition the existence of life. Kirilov, cites Charles, "takes a pistol in good Russian fashion and blows his brains out" to prove that he is God. He chose whether life existed or not. "Atheism," Charles writes, "is not liberation from God, it is not birth from God, it is letting one's self be divinized and absolutized and captured by that power which we call the Divine or God, in fact, enslaved by him, in the way of demonic possession, for by seeking to dominate God, you soak up divinity like a sponge soaks up water, so that you become God and you have to suffer all the consequences of this August position." [1]

When man tries to be God (with a capital "G") this prevents man from realizing his own humanity. Only by realizing his own humanity can he be moved toward true divinization, true theosis. The point is not to realize God's divinity, but to realize your own humanity, only then can reunion with God take place. To be born from God means to have a clear understanding of the nature of

God and man. They are distinct from one another, the creator and the created. They are bifurcated and need to experience reunion. In order to be reunited, both need to be fully realized and developed as they are intended. God is already fully realized. God is God. God, in turn, wants us to be fully developed as well, through our humanity. This desire by God is manifested in the freedom that we have as human beings. The freedom, in other words is the proof that God wants us to develop our personalities fully. This is the love that God has for us. It is a liberating love. Charles writes, "Once you love someone truly, you are liberated from him and if he loves you he is liberated from you. To be born from God means to enter into a loving relationship with Him. In love, each accepts the other for what he is. You want God to be God, for God wants you to be a human being. You don't fear God as the enemy of your humanity, on the contrary, you consider Him as its protector because He is the lover of man. God, you realize, is not a threat to your humanity but its source." 2

Charles points out that much of the history of religion involves the problem of "how to get God off your back." He remarks that much of the ritual, doctrine and ethics revolve around the central problem of keeping God from encroaching upon man's freedom. Yet Charles believes that within Christianity itself there is a unique and revolutionary aspect to the relationship between God and humanity; namely God gives us all the freedom we could want by entering into a loving relationship with us as individuals. Love, God's love for us, is at the foundation of our freedom. (Psalm 8)

Charles cites the parable of the prodigal son as the greatest commentary on this issue of freedom, its source and intention. God gives us this freedom and it is essentially, a test as to how we respond to it. We have two ways of responding. The first way is to be ungrateful, taking the freedom we have as our's to possess and discard. The other option is to respond with gratitude, offering back to God the richness of freedom He gave to us. Our gratitude results in sharing back with God what He has given us. In that moment, Charles says, "you become interdependent and therefore free from each other, for true freedom is interdependence." [3]

Notes to Birth Two

1. Ashanin, Charles. *The Problem of the Three Births of Man* p 3,4.

2. Ashanin, Charles. *The Problem of the Three Births of Man* p 4.

3. Ashanin, Charles. *The Problem of the Three Births of Man* p 6.

Birth Three

It is within this section of his most profound work that he speaks of his debt toward the existentialists, both on an academic and spiritual level. The third birth which Gregory of Nazianzus speaks of is making clean God's image in each of us through "tears and sufferings." Charles describes this as being "man's birth from himself, or man's liberation from himself." In the mythological fashion of a threshold guardian, Charles remarks, "this indeed is the most difficult enterprise." [1]

The movement toward freedom, this interdependence through objectification, continues on the inward journey within a human being. As the births or thresholds have been passed, as Jesus describes in Luke 12:49-51, the threshold of the self looms larger than the previous two. Jesus says in Matthew 10:34 that the Kingdom of Heaven is to be taken by force. This journey inward, the journey of the discovered self takes intentional and consistent effort. This effort manifests itself in the ability to stay awake (Luke 12:35-40) on the psychic level, staying on guard. Yet to be attentive, one has to be looking for something or for someone, specifically.

Charles first came across the articulation of this focus within the prophetic genius of the works of Dostoevsky at the Monastery at Praskvitza. Charles refers to the Apostle Paul as well as Shakespeare who bring up the issue of selfhood. Charles writes, "under the conditions of human existence and its fragmentation, man's image as he understands it appears broken and fragmented. You know you say to someone, do not fight yourself, but accept yourself and he tells you a profound truth--which of the many me's shall I choose and accept [?]" A human being, according to Charles, is not a singular, unified self. Rather, a human being exists as a collection of fragmented selves, giving the appearance of unity because of one voice, one body. In addition, this fragmented self lives in a fallen world where the good and the evil are mixed, what Boris Mouravieff calls "the mixtus orbis." [3]

In "A Garland for a Mother," Charles speaks of Perun and the pre-Christian ethos which greatly influenced his understanding of the relationship between the Slavic people and Christianity itself. [4] Charles understood that Christianity had roots within other cultures, which had other cosmologies. When Christianity came upon the scene, it did not do so by reinventing the wheel. It was molded and shaped by the people and their environment, since a religion is there to help reconcile a people to their environment. Therefore Charles understood that Christianity was not born in a cultural and mythological vacuum. It was born and grew with diverse and intricate influences.

A rich and largely unknown source of pre-Christian influences are indeed from the pre-Christian religion of the Slavs. [5] They had, according to Mouravieff, an especially unique and influential view of the problem of evil. Mouravieff writes,

The idea of Evil was conceived by them not in the abstract but in the concrete and empirical form. Not finding a place for Evil in a providential theogony, yet seeing Evil act in life side by side with the Good, the Slavs recognized its divine origin and nature and personified it with the name of *Tchernobog* (the black God). [6]

It seems that the Slavs, these ancestors of the Serbs, made a unique attempt to reconcile the presence of evil in a world created by a good God. They did not take the dualistic concept, such as the Persian viewpoint of Ormuzd and Ahriman. Neither did they take the viewpoint which eventually developed within Judaeo-Christianity which says that evil acts as a sort of deviation from the divine Will, which sides with the Good, " . . . in other words, it admits a transgression of the divine Will which after this fact appears somewhat *limited*." 7

The Slavs saw Evil (*Tchernobog*) acting within its own environment, the Earth, under the authority of the Son of God (*Svarogitch*). This allowed them to see the supreme God (*Svarog*) as the absolute authority within the universe who "does not admit [the existence of] Evil. Neither does he recognize it. But as it nonetheless exists, *He neither looks at it nor speaks of it* . . ." signifying ". . . that *the supreme God did not want to see human sins, and that by ignoring their existence He let them pass in silence*." 9

The Slavs perceived of the supreme God as only dealing with the celestial realm, his influences not reaching the realm of the Earth.

In a remarkable interview with Bob (10/5), Charles speaks extensively about the "Energies of God." In this talk, he says that the uncreated energies of God are "peculiar to the Divine being." He says that these energies are pre-existent and created within God, yet brought into action *outside* of God. He says that there are certain energies which are particular to that being, which cannot be communicated because "*God lives in his own sanctity.*" These energies are sent out from God as a way of God calling to the world *outside* of Himself. These energies which are sent out from God are the *created* energies, yet they are not God Himself. They are an "outflow from God."

Here, Charles gives us a hint as to the influence of the pre-Christian religion of the Slavs. He himself sees his Triune Christian God as existing supremely outside of the influence of the Earthly realm, "living in his own sanctity." He understood that the God of Heaven was indeed the absolute and supreme God who was in control of everything. This meant that He did not allow for evil to have any freedom to work in the earthly realm alone. Charles saw God as the ultimate Will in the Universe, allowing for this freedom (which Dostoevsky helped him understand) to choose between the good and evil. God wants us to choose the good, but that is not always the case. Yet God never allows for the evil to run rampant, unabated. Evil is on a mission, a mission to see the return of God to Himself. God's desire is for the safe return of all of his "particles" to

Himself. This return is a process, a lifelong process of salvation. Charles considers this process to be a training, an education. In Coalson Interview 2/17 he says, "a sincere Christian is always training himself for death . . . death is a test. It is a problem, an encounter with the higher consciousness . . . the Spirit of this great liberator that we call Jesus Christ."

Life is all about the return to God. God allows this world to be a mixture of good and evil in order to fuel our return back to Him. Charles was never frightened of evil itself. He was frightened of losing his way back to God. Charles was frightened of not passing this test, this lifelong examination of how we live. For him, the passing of the test was not what one said, but how one acted.

The human psyche lives in this 'mixtus orbis' in a fragmented condition with an endless supply of obstacles. Yet all of these obstacles within this human existence have one goal in mind; to see to it that this particle is returned to God in its original condition.

Within the fragmented human psyche is planted the seeds of consciousness (Luke 8:4-15). This consciousness begins to grow naturally through an examination of one's place within the universe. Many times this consciousness begins to arise when the world around you stops making "sense" and the circumstances of life no longer meet the expectations of life. You realize you are not controlling life's circumstances, they are controlling you. Mouravieff calls this a state of "moral bankruptcy." Charles refers to this when he says "man's trouble is that he is inflicted with something which he did not choose--existence. Existence has chosen you and me, rather than we ourselves choosing it. Now being thrown into existence, man suffers anxiety because he does not know what to do with existence because it presents him so many choices and possibilities . . . so existentialists tell us how to solve the problem. You must make a decision." [10]

This quote encapsulates much of the philosophy behind the decision which Charles made regarding his lifelong exile. It explains his amazing sense of attention toward his goal of passing the test of existence and returning back to God. The author heard Charles refer numerous times to the importance of this issue of decision. He would often times remark that a poor decision is much better than no decision at all (Revelation 3:15-16). Within the act of decision-making, energy is focused, preserved and built up. This "psychic" energy is invaluable as it is essentially the fuel that drives the movement through these three thresholds, the three births. This act of decision-making opens doors of wisdom within oneself, far beyond the scope of the wisdom grounded solely in the intellect. The wisdom of this world is too "sophisticated," according to Charles. It is not wisdom available to the common person. When he uses the term "sophisticated," he means this in terms of wisdom created by and for the intellectuals themselves. Charles defines intellectuals here as "people bent on proving that it is only their own philosophy that makes sense and everyone else's is nonsense." [11]

This myopic attitude essentially causes human wisdom to cancel its self out. When wisdom arises solely from the head without the heart contributing and balancing, then the result is an answer designed for that person only. Not only is it designed for them only, but it is also atheistic in nature, as defined in Charles' essay "The Problem of the Three Births of Man." When the intellect acts alone it essentially places itself in position of the Divine. It seeks to dominate God by acting in God's place. This in effect is a demonic issue, for it isolates man from his own humanity within himself by seeking the powers of creation, which only God can administer effectively. God gives human beings the freedom to realize our true nature within our own humanity through our personalities, as well as within our own divine nature as Jesus Christ revealed. Yet God does not give us this freedom in order to overtake Him. We are to become co-creators, not creators. When we attempt to become creators, then this isolates us even further from our own human nature as well as the collective human nature as community.

Charles reveals to us how closely he was in rhythm with the twentieth and twenty-first centuries when he asks the question of how to achieve these births. The answer given for centuries was to abandon the milieu of the social world and renounce it, renounce the world, renounce the body and dedicate one's existence to attaining theosis. But Charles felt that this path is impractical for the vast majority of people in today's modern world. Charles sees the description of this new birth as

man's acceptance of the fact that he is not the center of the universe, a self-made creation who worships his creator, but rather that he is created to seek himself in God in whom his true self is to be seen. Through this act man comprehends himself and the universe as meaningful only in relation to God, their creator.

In that act, man grasps the shattering and yet most healing and saving fact, that this existence makes sense not in relationship to itself primarily, but to God and because it is related to God, it is centered in Him, and man, perceiving the truth of this vision and accepting it, frees his hold on himself and frees himself from himself and is like a prisoner who has thrown off his chains and his prison and entered a new world of infinite freedom, no longer anxious as to what he will eat or drink or wherewith he will be clothed, for he realizes that God, his Maker, already knows these things. [12]

When a human being allows himself or herself to be used as an instrument, this guarantees a reaction from God. Charles says "this knowledge releases his energy for true creativeness, because he no longer holds himself captive to himself, but makes himself an available instrument, no longer for his own purposes, but for God's . . ." [13]

These passages touch the heart of Charles' theology and cosmology. He was one of the rare human beings who allowed himself to be completely taken over by God and remade in His image. He sacrificed his life with his immediate family in Montenegro in order to work at developing his personality to its fullest. He did not play by the rules of Western society. He listened to the rhythm of an ancient civilization which was never fully born. It was a civilization which was intent upon the full development, both mind, body and spirit of a human being. Our Western Civilization, in its current form, almost completely ignores the development of the emotional center, the heart. This has left us blindly following our five senses with a fragmented psyche, completely unprepared to guard its holy particle of Christ from the isolating and destructive nature of this fallen world.

Notes to Birth Three

1. Ashanin, Charles. *The Problem of the Three Births* p 6.

2. Ashanin, Charles. *The Problem of the Three Births* p 7.

3. Mouravieff, Boris. *Gnosis: Book Two; Mesoteric Cycle* Praxis Institute Press. Translated by S.A. Wissa, Manek d'Oncieu and Robin Amis, ed by Robin Amis, 1992 p 131.

4. Ashanin, Charles. "A Garland for a Mother," p 140.

5. Mouravieff, p 134.

6. Mouravieff, p 134.

7, Mouravieff, p 134.

8. Mouravieff, Boris. *The Beliefs of the Pre-Christian Slavs* Praxis Monograph Number Four. Praxis Research Institute, Inc. 2001 p 9.

9. Mouravieff, Boris. *The Beliefs of the Pre-Christian Slavs* p 8.

10. Ashanin, Charles. *The Problem of the Three Births* p 7.

11. Ashanin, Charles. *The Problem of the Three Births* p 8.

12. Ashanin, Charles. *The Problem of the Three Births* p 8.

13. Ashanin, Charles. *The Problem of the Three Births* p 8.

A Theology of Uncreated Energies

We are a depository of energy of its own kind.

-- Charles to Bob (Interview 10/5)

Charles had "the unearthly ability to live in the fallen world as one redeemed." He did so by focusing on his mission as this spiritual soldier dropped behind enemy lines, all the while searching for like-hearted allies. This unwavering focus was evidence that he had a link with God beyond his relationship to his family, tribe, profession, religious organization and social status. He lived in relationship to God, as the created does toward the creator. For him God was his source of his true desires and needs. This meant that Charles had come in contact with God in some form, over a period of time. This form of God Charles and his Cappadocian colleagues would term "the uncreated energies of God."

This is the way the early church fathers described the *knowability* of God. God cannot be known through God's essence. God can only be known through God's energies. St. Gregory of Nyssa used the analogy of the sun emitting its rays. The energies are felt, yet to know their source is impossible and destructive to the naked eye. [1] The essence of God the creator is far too marvelous for our undeveloped personalities to comprehend. In Coalson Interview 10/5, Charles speaks extensively about the energies of God. He says that there is a vast difference between what is known as the uncreated and the created energies of God. The uncreated energies are God himself. This is a completely different realm than the earthly realm. It is not accessible to the world. God cannot be seen, however God can be seen in his created acts or energies. In other words, there is a vast difference between who God is (uncreated energies) and what God created (created energies). He says to Bob,

> Many people substitute what God created for God himself. We discern God by entering mystically . . . there is something hidden within us, we call it the soul, which somehow [is] aware of God as a mystery and we communicated with that mystery by plunging into ourselves, chiefly through prayer,

> whereby the spirit of God in ourselves resonate to each other.

These two levels of God, which George Maloney remarks that St. Gregory of Palamas referred to as God's higher and lower, superior and inferior levels. 2 God's energies or love permeates our being, awakens our potentialities and gives us the drive toward actualization. This actualization is called theosis or divinization and is not realized unless the development of the whole person is addressed by the individual, family and society through a process of re-education, i.e. Christian Humanism.

God has a plan for each of us and for all of humanity and creation. God needs us to realize our true nature. God wants us back, back in his presence. We are particles of Christ, destined to be reunited as one body. This life is the arduous journey back to God. Charles was a guide, leading those who were willing, back toward God. Charles himself described himself as a "quarryman" whose job it was to select stones for the artist to sculpt (Coalson 2-17-00). But this leading back was only to a point. These three births which Gregory of Nazianzus points out and Charles elaborates upon are only attainable through personal struggle, suffering and sacrifice. Even yet, to the pilgrim, the energies of

God are detected within the suffering. They are like a voice in the wooded wilderness calling the pilgrim back toward the path. This voice of God is not easily detected. Our fallen psyches in this fallen world prevent our clear understanding. It is an acquired ability, this listening. This listening is called prayer. Without prayer, without the ability to listen, even the best intentions lay wasted on the forest floor. For Charles, prayer is not talking, "prayer is listening, listening, listening." It takes effort, repeated effort to acquire the ability to listen. We must be wise in the ways of the journey. We must know the terrain and the traits of the enemy. We must be alert at all times. We must constantly be able to adjust to the fluidness of this fallen world. Most importantly we must always be aware of the nature of the journey itself, this journey back to God.

This journey is the ultimate journey. It is the highest calling of a human being, this divinization. It also contains the highest risk for the human species, what Jesus termed the sin against the holy spirit. Jesus says in Mark 3:28-29, "Believe me, all men's sins can be forgiven and all their blasphemies. But there can never be any forgiveness for blasphemy against the Holy Spirit. That is an eternal sin." This knowledge, this hidden, inner knowledge is contained within each one of us. By its very nature it is unforgiving. Once you have understood the nature of your true self and its divinity, there is literally no other path than full actualization, divinization, theosis. The destruction of the temporal flesh is nothing compared to eternal torment of an unreliable soul, essentially an aborted spirit caught in the void between the evolving animal and the new creature in Christ.

This is the clearest clue as to why Charles Ashanin was such a driven man. He had seen too much. He had seen within himself the divine particle of Christ, the cosmic link offering reunion with the Father. For him, there was absolutely no turning back. By the age of twenty-four he had seen enough to cause him to leave his family and his church, his future profession, his homeland, his entire known universe and plunge headlong into the darkness of exile. He had no tangible signposts, no direction other than the Displaced Persons Camps in Italy. His real direction came from within, this homeland in the soul. He had discovered within himself a reality that loomed larger than the pain of exile. Yet this pain, this suffering left its scar.

His entire life must be seen from this one-way journey back to God, which involved his entire being. Everything and everybody in his life fit into his own completion of this journey. Everything and everybody revolved around his personality being a consistent and loyal instrument for the Divine. The desires of Charles

Bozidar Ashanin longed for the desires of God. The only thing that mattered was for him to be useful, to function as he was designed. Charles used all of his freedom that God had given him as fuel for this epic journey back to God. This journey manifested itself in his outer, social and professional world as a teacher. For Charles, his students were not just students. His students were Christ personified. He nurtured them, seeking out the good, true nature in each one. He sought for those who were willing and able to listen to the internal, divine call that he had heard and responded to. For those who did not hear this distinctive call, he nurtured them just the same, as Jesus says in Luke 17:1-3a,

> It is inevitable that there should be pitfalls, but alas for the man who is responsible for them! It would be better for that man to have a millstone hung round his neck and be thrown into the sea, than that he should trip up one of these little ones. So be careful how you live. (NRSV)

Charles was careful, very careful. His students were his hire and he was determined to be worthy of his hire, as Mouravieff says. His students, indeed were Christ to him. He cared little about jumping through the academic hoops or keeping pace with the social etiquette of the West. His task was not to please men or an institution. His task was to be an instrument, consistent and loyal to the Almighty God who lived in him, who breathed life into him and sustained his every movement. These were movements of spirit as well as the body. With each incident of attention toward the Divine element within him, he gained more and more energy from the Divine. He believed that these energies were the overflow of God himself. He said to Bob (10/5), "the closer you are to God, the more created energies are produced. The created energies aren't there to transform the world, but to enter into the sacred space or spirit of God." He interpreted the miracles of Jesus as not being God himself, but the created energies or the by-product of God.

This energy the ancients termed "love." This word has clearly lost its meaning in our present age, yet it remains as the sharpest description of the energy of God, the energy needed in order to return successfully to God. Paul speaks most clearly about this in I Corinthians 13.

This successful return has an implicit quality to it: dignity. It is the quality which flows from the heart of a human being who has discovered and consistently maintained their holy integrity. This holy integrity is defined as the listening to the inner call of the

Divine. Charles spent his entire adult life consistently maintaining this link between his being and the Being of God, for as Christ promises, "the man who has something will receive more." (Mark 4:25a) It was through this link that allowed him to sustain his exile, through the loss of his exile, its loneliness. He left his family in Montenegro exposed to the influence of the evil one. For Charles, this was his suffering. Through his suffering he was privileged enough to existentially experience his own Golgotha, as Jesus Christ experienced. Suffering, as Charles understood it and experienced it was the gateway to the Divine within the human soul. In a 1988 video interview with his dear friend Ted Nottingham, Charles soars as he speaks of the Orthodox understanding of suffering. He says

The cross has been interpreted in our Western thought (and in Orthodox thought inasmuch as it is influenced by this theological legalism) as representing God's punishment for our sins. But there is another aspect to the Cross, which Orthodox believers emphasize: while suffering is there, the suffering is not seen as God's punishment, but as the way in which He is begetting (like a mother in travail) sons and daughters into His glory. [3]

For Charles, "the way of suffering is the way of salvation." He continues, 'this is the way in which God redeems His world. We might say that suffering is the begetting of Christ within each one of us, but this occurs only when our suffering is accepted as a way of transformation or what Teilhard de Chardin called "Christique." It is the formation of Christ within us.' [4] This experience of suffering of the three births must be participated in fully by us. The acceptance of suffering is in effect the turning point. We all suffer, yet it is our acceptance of this suffering that gives us ears to hear. Charles was faced with his exile, his suffering, his Golgotha. At age twenty-four he stood at the cross road of his evolution and had to decide whether or not he was going to participate in the true nature which God intended for him, which God intends for the entire universe. Charles realized that God, the God of the universe, needed him because through him God could transform this universe into what God intended. Charles realized that God wanted to *create through him*. Yet for this to happen, much suffering would occur and it needed to be accepted.

Through this acceptance of suffering, an intimate, personal relationship with the living God begins to form life. In the interview with Ted Nottingham, Charles says, "You cannot have a relationship with anyone without imposing upon your own life a demand of self-sacrifice. And this Holy God reveals Himself as

One who sacrifices Himself for us." [5] It is through God's initial sacrifice and our subsequent acceptance of our suffering which triggers this process of transformation or *Christique*. This transformation produces faith. There is no such thing as blind faith.

The faith of Charles Ashanin was based upon his experience of a living, dynamic God. His God was not one based loosely in a fragmented psyche prone to constant wandering. He had discovered a place of rest for God within himself, an inward sanctuary designed by God before Charles was born. This sanctuary he called his inward heart and nothing else dwelled there but God. Because of this, Charles had a unity about him that either attracted or repelled. There was no middle ground. This inward sanctuary allowed his body, mind and soul to act as one, not as *legion*. When you encountered Charles in whatever capacity, you encountered one person, not a legion masquerading as one. Charles was the type of human being whom God intended. He listened to God, allowing Him to shape his life. He did not will his life, he accepted it. Charles was Paul's new creature. Charles was the new man.

Notes to A Theology of Uncreated Energies

1. Maloney, George A, S. J. *A Theology of Uncreated Energies.* Marquette University Press, Milwaukee, Wisconsin, April 16, 1978, p 65.

2. Maloney, p 74.

3. Ashanin, Charles. "Turning Toward the Light," transcript page 17.

4. Ashanin, Charles. "Turning Toward the Light," transcript page 17.

5. Ashanin, Charles. "Turning Toward the Light," transcript page 8.

Epilogue

Obituary page D6, *Indianapolis Star*, Friday March 3, 2000

Services for **Charles B. Ashanin**, 79, Indianapolis, a retired professor of church history, will be at 10 a.m. March 4 in St. George Orthodox Christian Church, of which he was a member, with calling there from 4 to 8 p.m. March 3. Burial will be in Crown Hill Cemetery. He died March 1.

Mr. Ashanin was professor emeritus of church history at Christian Theological Seminary, which he taught for 23 years. He retired in 1990.

A graduate of Glasgow University, Scotland, he also had studied in England and taught at the University of Ghana in Legon, Africa, and at Allen and Claflin Universities in South Carolina.

He was described as a wise man whom students, their friends and friends of friends, sought out for counseling even after he retired from teaching.

"His empathy with students of all types, kinds and ages was remarkable," one of his students wrote to the Indianapolis Star in 1995. "His experiences, depth of study, concern for the sheer value of life and its living radiates throughout his lectures, his conversations, his suggestions and his guidance."

We are here for a purpose," Mr. Ashanin told the *Star* that same year. "I'm seeking daily to see what I have to do to contribute to that purpose. That's what keeps me ticking--the divine purpose of my own life."

Born in Yugoslavia, Mr. Ashanin graduated from Cetinje Seminary during the Nazi occupation, later joined the resistance movement against the communists and then escaped to Italy.

"I have experienced anguish beyond measure because I went through the German occupation. I went through the Communist persecution," he said. "I have been a pilgrim who has gone thousands of miles, so to speak, through the desert."

He said he found inspiration in the words of writers such as Feodor Mikhailovich Dostoevski and Leo Nikolayevich Tolstoy.

"I turn to the experiences of human beings who have managed to overcome despair and the way they have found to not only survive, but to live in confidence," he said. "Whatever happens to us human beings, there is something ahead of us, what the mystics call the fulfillment or the transcendent promise that God will conquer the evil in us . . . "

Made in the USA
San Bernardino, CA
06 August 2017